LIVING ON THE HOME FRONT

LIVING ON THE HOME FRONT

MEGAN WESTLEY

AMBERLEY

For Benjamin, my ever-fixed mark, whose constant support and encouragement makes anything seem possible, whether in the 1940s or the present day. In memory of corned beef lunches, wartime tantrums and the unwavering belief that it would all come together in the end.

First published 2013

Amberley Publishing
The Hill, Stroud
Gloucestershire, GL5 4EP

www.amberley-books.com

British Library Cataloguing in Publication Data.
A catalogue record for this book is available from the British Library.

ISBN 978-1-4456-0453-4

Typeset in 11pt on 14pt Sabon.
Typesetting and Origination by Amberley Publishing.
Printed in the UK.

Contents

Introduction

Even now, as I sit down to compose this introduction after completing the book you are about to read, I find it hard to believe that the last twelve months really happened.

Digging the victory garden, running for cover at the sudden sound of an air-raid siren, measuring out a week's rations – these activities conjure up sepia-toned images of times long gone by, when life was very different and our modern society was a distant dream. For me, these things are viewed in a more contemporary light. Over a year ago, I decided that I wanted to explore, in depth, what it was like to live on the Second World War 'Home Front' in Britain. Not only did I want to write about it; I wanted to experience it first-hand. I decided to stop wondering, and start doing.

When I told people that I was about to spend a year living on wartime rations and 'making do', most of them thought that I was insane. Many still do when I tell them about it now. Such a strange display of masochism is, to some, hard to fathom. There is a small part of me that agrees, and feels that the experiment was odd at best; ludicrous at times. Nevertheless, it happened, and I had good reasons for wanting to do it.

The Modern Day

Modern society is a fiercely criticised thing. To its detractors, it is wasteful, violent, consumerist, selfish, immoral. To say that all of these descriptions are true is to turn ourselves over to cynicism; however, they cannot be ignored entirely. It has for some time been my belief –

and the belief of many others, particularly among the older generation – that society and life might have been healthier in the past.

Consumerism, although by no means a new thing, seems to have gone mad since the 1940s. Millions of people now live far beyond their means in order to keep up with the latest 'must have' purchases. While some of these purchases are useful and valued, many are entirely pointless. Credit cards and pay-day loans provide short-term assistance, but ultimately long-term debt. In the middle of a recession, we all have less money but are encouraged to keep spending in order to keep the nation's economy going. Once the spiral of debt has begun, it becomes very hard to escape it. The sheer number of 'things' we have nowadays, compared to the average wartime person, is quite incredible. Every occasion requires a new outfit, gadgets control every room in the house and more things are disposable. We 'upgrade' perfectly good and working items in order to have something better without even thinking about why. This is not a display of finger-pointing on my part; I am as guilty as the next person. For whole generations of society, this is just how things are.

Such a large number of things leads inevitably to a large amount of waste. This isn't simply a waste of clothes, appliances and household items. Energy and water are high on the list of wasted products. Food wastage is also happening on a grand scale, as we all buy far more than we need and throw away whatever is left over. This can be down to many things – oversized portions, shopping for products we don't realise we already have at home, poor meal planning, not date checking, impulse buying; the list could go on. With so much food on offer, many of us are getting fatter. This isn't only due to the quantity of what is consumed, but also the quality of it. Fast food is a growing industry, as cheap and easy meals take priority in busy working lives. Not only are an excess of food and higher amounts of waste bad for the economy, they're also bad for the environment.

Producing the amount of food that could potentially be eaten in the UK uses a lot of energy. Resources are used to grow, feed and harvest crops, to care for animals and to prepare, transport and store the finished products. The situation wouldn't be as bad if the food eaten in Britain was all produced in Britain, but a large proportion of it is not. Add the environmental cost of flying food halfway around the world, and an ugly picture begins to take shape.

There are also broader social criticisms thrown at the modern world. It's said that people are less involved in what is going on around them: community involvement sinks lower on our list of priorities and anti-social behaviour increases.

The Year to Come

Setting aside these arguments, whether we agree with them or not, one question still lingers: why, if I am piqued by curiosity, should I choose to live on the home front for a whole year? Why not a few months? I toyed with the idea of dedicating just one month of my time to researching and living each year of the war, in order to track the changes that took place in rationing as the war years went by. I'd be living through all the events, but within a shorter timescale. In the end, I decided that seven months (for the seven years from 1939 to 1945) wasn't enough for me to really appreciate what the home front would have been like. Measures such as rationing would have become harder as time went on. In seven months, I might have only just begun to flag before my time was up. Somehow, a year seemed harder and more convincing. In all honesty, however, I couldn't contemplate spending any more than a year in the Second World War.

A year would allow me to experience all the seasons through the eyes of war: the times of relative plenty, when the vegetable patch was abundant with fresh produce, and the fallow months when the basic rations were all I'd have. It was also important to me to attempt to experience all the war years separately. The war didn't begin with one set of rationing rules and continue unchanged until VE Day in May 1945. Initially, in 1939, there was no food rationing at all. As the many months went by until peace was announced, the allowance of food, clothing and furniture constantly changed as amounts increased or decreased and more items were added to the list. The end result of my experiment, as you will see, is a diary in which the years of the war are scaled down to fit within my one year. The war years of 1939 and 1945 were essentially half-years, 1939 beginning in September and 1945 ending in May. To replicate these years, I spent one month living in each of them. The five remaining full years of the war, from 1940 to 1944, were each allocated two months.

The real home front was forged in the fires of war and necessity – to contemplate applying the principles generated during that period in a modern setting was difficult. But the self-denial in terms of food wasn't necessarily harder than following one of the faddish diets you see in magazines today; perhaps it just lasted a little longer than a fad diet.

I'm well aware that my experience was different to that of the average 1930s–40s person. I don't try to claim that this experiment could in any way replicate the fear and hardship of the actual home front. Not only did their experience of the war cover many more years, but it also came with the added negatives of air raids, bombings, separation, fear for loved ones and loss. I could never know how it might feel to be a mother sending her child away to live with strangers in the countryside, or to be a young woman whose husband is called away to fight with no guarantee of return. I also don't know how it would feel to spend sleepless night after sleepless night in a cold, damp Anderson shelter in the garden and then emerge in the morning to enter a house with no gas or water due to bomb damage, before heading out to work a long, hard day in a munitions factory. I have nothing but admiration for those people, all of them, who lived through the war.

It is also important to point out that in this book I have not attempted to convey in any great detail the experience of those living in other countries. Conditions varied so much that to attempt to do so in the time allocated would be unsuccessful and, most likely, highly inaccurate. My intention is merely to tell one side of the story – that of the British – though the hardships of others should certainly not be forgotten. For the most part, civilians were, after all, simply civilians: somebody's wife, mother, father, son, trying to carry on with life. Armies may go to war, but there are always people left behind.

The only advantage that the real wartime community had over me during the course of my experiment was the community itself. At times, being the only person living with rationing, separated from the distractions and comforts of the modern world, could be an incredibly lonely experience. What got me through some of the tougher times was the support of my family and friends, who didn't necessarily always know how I felt, but were happy to listen to me moan about it. Some of them even joined in at strategic points to help me along. There is no greater marker of a good companion than one who is willing to eat wartime rations with you.

It may be useful if I explain briefly what my 'modern-day' life is like; or was like before I began the wartime year. In many respects, I am a fairly typical woman in my mid-20s. I have a wardrobe full of clothes (but frequently claim I have 'nothing to wear') and the things I use most during an average day are a laptop computer and the television. If given the opportunity, I can waste hours at a time on the internet and not be able to pin down what I've actually done. I live in Cornwall, so have a fairly rural way of life, and already grow a small selection of vegetables in my back garden. Some of the characters most likely to crop up in the diary entries of this book are my sister Lauren (whom I rent a house with), my partner Benjamin and my friends Becky and Aaron. In sum, my life is fairly normal.

Let us now go back. It's 1939. Glenn Miller reigns supreme in the world of music, and Merle Oberon and Laurence Olivier have just starred in *Wuthering Heights*. Neville Chamberlain is the Prime Minister of Great Britain. It's a warm Sunday morning in early September, and I turn on the wireless to catch up on events when I hear a life-changing and dramatic announcement.

The Phoney War (February)

I am speaking to you from the Cabinet Room at 10 Downing Street. This morning the British Ambassador in Berlin handed the German Government a final note stating that, unless we heard from them by 11 o'clock that they were prepared at once to withdraw their troops from Poland, a state of war would exist between us. I have to tell you now that no such undertaking has been received, and that consequently this country is at war with Germany. You can imagine what a bitter blow it is to me that all my long struggle to win peace has failed. Yet I cannot believe that there is anything more or anything different that I could have done and that would have been more successful.

British Prime Minister Neville Chamberlain announces the declaration of war in a radio broadcast, on 3 September, 1939.

As Chamberlain informed the nation, just over two hours earlier, at 9.00 a.m. on 3 September, 1939, the British Ambassador had presented the German Foreign Secretary with a note stating that the British Government's instructions had not been followed; despite sending an ultimatum over 24 hours earlier, Germany's attacks on Poland had not desisted, but had instead continued and intensified. The note concluded that unless a change was made by 11 a.m. British Summer Time, war would begin between the two countries. When no such promise was made, the Prime Minister was forced to accept the fact that hostilities were inevitable.

This is where I enter the story; at around 11.15 a.m. on 3 September. Reading the newspaper reports of the following day, I believe Chamberlain when he expresses his deep regret about the situation. The

Government consoled itself with knowledge of the attempts it had made at a peaceful resolution to the unrest. On the morning of the declaration, Winston Churchill, First Lord of the Admiralty in the War Cabinet, spoke out: 'Outside, the storms of war may blow and the land may be lashed with the fury of its gales, but in our own hearts, this Sunday morning, there is peace. Our hands may be active, but our consciences are at rest.'

In 1939

31 March: Britain and France announce their support of Poland, which is in fierce negotiations with Germany over land.

1 April: The Spanish Civil War, which began in July 1936, ends.

4 April: A mutual assistance pact is signed between Britain and Poland.

27 April: The Military Training Act is passed in Britain. Under this, all fit and able men aged 20–21 were required to undertake six months' military training.

3 June: In an article within *Collier's* magazine, Winston Churchill states that he believes Germany is keen to 'make war' before the end of the year. On the same day, over 200,000 men aged 20–21 are called up to fight in the event of war.

11 August: A 'trial run' for the blackout takes place.

23 August: Germany and the USSR sign a non-aggression pact.

31 August: The British Royal Navy becomes on full alert and mobilisation of the Army and Navy begins. In Germany, a radio broadcast outlines a peace plan that has allegedly been refused by Poland.

1 September: German troops invade Poland. In Britain, the evacuation

of 3,000,000 women and children from densely populated towns and cities begins and blackout restrictions are put in place. The Army and Royal Air Force are officially mobilised.

3 September: Britain and France declare war on Germany, and British Prime Minister Neville Chamberlain announces this to the nation through a radio broadcast. The internment of those living in Britain with 'enemy' nationality starts; many are moved to camps on the Isle of Man.

9 September: In a Cabinet meeting, Chamberlain prepares for a three-year war.

10 September: Canada declares war on Germany.

16 September: Petrol is rationed. To obtain ration books, drivers must apply for them at their local post office or tax office.

27 September: The wartime budget is announced, with income tax rising to the highest ever rate of 7s 6d in every pound; a two-shilling rise from the tax rate announced in April.

14 October: The British battleship HMS *Royal Oak* is torpedoed and sunk by a German submarine off the coast of Scotland. 833 of the 1,234 men on board are killed.

21 October: Conscription begins for men aged 20–23. Men aged 18 and 19 are not immediately called up, amid concern about the strain felt by younger soldiers on the front line.

11 November: In a broadcast, Queen Elizabeth, wife of King George VI, calls for women to join the war effort.

13 November: Eight bombs are dropped on the Shetland Islands by German aircraft. Four fall on the land, making this the first bombing on British soil in the Second World War. The remaining four bombs fall in the sea, and nobody is injured.

Preparations for War

By September 1939, most civilians had been issued with gas masks in preparation for war. Gas had been such a popular weapon in the First World War that its use was a major fear. Hand rattles were issued to air-raid wardens and people were told that if they heard the rattle being used they should put on their gas masks immediately. A special gas-proof pram was designed to protect young babies. A singularly unstylish item, it resembled an airtight coffin with a small window in the top and a chimney and gas filter, to allow air to enter it. A rubber pump at one end could be squeezed at regular intervals to release stale air from inside the pram and inject fresh air through the gas filter. Despite such precautions – or perhaps because of them – gas was never used as a weapon against the civilian population. Some believe that Hitler, learning of the widespread gas-mask distribution in Britain, simply felt that there was no point spending money and energy on such a weapon.

The 'Dig for Victory' campaign, encouraging those with free land (including gardens) to grow their own food, began in October 1939. In a radio broadcast on 3 October, Sir Reginald Dorman-Smith, the Minister for Agriculture, appealed to people to begin producing for themselves, stating that a further 500,000 allotments worked could cater for an additional 1,000,000 adults and 1,500,000 children, for eight months out of the year. An initial problem was locating enough land to put this into practice. Green spaces on the outskirts of towns and cities, including potential building sites, were given over to vegetables. One example given to motivate others was the area of Bishopsdown Park, in Tunbridge Wells. Here, the park was divided into allotment spaces for the use of residents surrounding it.

Not long after war was announced, the National Registration Act was passed and National Identity Cards were issued to every person in the United Kingdom. It was important that these cards were looked after, as they could be requested as proof of identity and legally had to be produced. These allowed for the effective administration of rationing, as identity could be proven, and also provided an additional measure against spies and foreign 'aliens'. Each card contained details of the holder's name, address, age, date of birth, sex, occupation and marital status. In October 1939, 65,000 people were employed specially for the distribution of identity cards.

The Early Stages

Food rationing didn't begin until January 1940, so in the first month of my experiment my diet will be that of a typical 1930s person. Food is relatively plentiful, but what I eat must be seasonal and made from scratch.

One challenge I have effectively forgotten about is washing. I am no longer able to use our washing machine and tumble dryer, and must instead do everything by hand. This is no great bother, but means that the process will take far longer than I am used to. I don't have a washboard or mangle either, so will have to scrub and wring my clothes as well as possible with my hands. An experience to be put off, I feel.

Bathing is another job to be revolutionised. During the war, people were encouraged to use as little water as possible. Baths were kept to a depth of 5 inches, and to observe this strictly many householders drew a thick black line around their tub with paint. Sensing that this is one suggestion that would not be well received in the house, I will instead attempt to perfect this by eye (with a ruler for help).

One public information film broadcast in 1939, entitled 'Household Hints in War', advises against waste of any kind. Viewers are asked to stop dripping taps, reuse cinders from a fire, turn off lights when not needed and avoid wasting gas by leaving kettles boiling. A sharp voice instructs, 'Don't waste food. There is enough for all, but not enough to waste!' This vendetta against waste continued throughout the war, as the nation became more frugal and learned to 'make do and mend'.

The message concludes with a note of positivity – 'It's beginning to sound as if you mustn't do anything, but just for a change here is a "do".' This 'do' centres on a wedding. In fact, many people took up the advice. The number of weddings in August and September 1939 reached a record high.

Propaganda

As the war progressed, propaganda became an important weapon. A variety of posters were distributed to warn people of the best ways to behave during hostilities. Any information received from a loved one in the forces should be treated with the strictest confidence. With German spies everywhere (or, at least, the possibility of them), the firm message was that you could never know who might be listening in on a conversation.

A 1939 poster aimed at troops on leave showed two men talking, with one almost giving away the location of his future posting in conversation: 'Blimey, I nearly said it!' Behind them, the wall has an ear, connected to a Nazi swastika. A well-known slogan with the same message was 'Careless talk costs lives'. Posters depicted people talking in a number of different situations, while unbeknown to them Adolf Hitler or prominent Nazis were nearby, waiting to pass on the information. 'Be like Dad, keep Mum' was a popular slogan within the 'careless talk' series. Introduced in 1940, it was later followed by a poster featuring a glamorous woman, with the instruction 'Keep Mum, she's not so dumb'. Others advised 'Tittle tattle lost the battle' and 'Keep it under your hat!' Though these warnings are now an accepted part of the war, at the time they were unpopular with some. The *Daily Telegraph* printed a column, criticising the government's apparent censorship of its own people. The 'careless talk' campaign was viewed as overly dramatic and a step too far for a 'free' society. While the public was willing to accept rationing of food, it was not quite as keen to embrace 'rationing of the tongue'.

Posters can be found relating to almost every aspect of home-front life. A number of them were simply morale boosting; one depicted Winston Churchill (after he became Prime Minister) with the message 'Let us go forward together'. Simple, everyday advice could be found on billboards. A 'Don't waste food!' advertisement advocated 'Better pot luck with Churchill today than humble pie under Hitler tomorrow'. Mothers were told 'Reinforce children's clothes – They will last twice as long'.

Defending the Home-Front Home

The threat of air raids was at the forefront of everyone's mind, and had been since before the war began. During the First World War, devastation caused by aerial attacks had been widespread and shocking. It was predicted by the RAF that up to 200,000 people could be killed or injured during just one week of bombing.

Air Raid Precautions (ARP) wardens were appointed and on 4 June, three months before the outbreak of war, the first practical exercise of the Westminster district took place. Wardens were fully equipped with items such as gas rattles, hand bells and anti-gas suits, which could be needed in the line of duty. Hand rattles would be used to warn of a gas attack, and bells used to indicate when the danger was over. On 6 June, the whole of London was subjected to a trial air raid. Although the event was designed only to test the effectiveness and audibility of the sirens, not to drill the public in sheltering, the test must have struck an unnerving note among those bracing themselves for the hardships to come.

In 1938, in preparation for war, literature was issued to every household, with instructions on 'The Protection of Your Home Against Air Raids'. People were advised to prepare their home for war long before it came. A key element of this protection was the designation of a 'refuge room' within the house, or within a number of flats. Ideally, the refuge room should be one that has small windows and faces another building or narrow street. If not, the windows of the room could be protected by sandbags or boxes of earth. The best option for a refuge room was a space in a basement or cellar; or at the least, a room not on the top floor of a house. This was because the floor above the room could then act as a further layer of protection if an incendiary bomb was dropped. To guard against incendiaries, it was advisable to have sand or earth to hand, which could be shovelled on top of the bomb to smother it. Those living in flats or shared houses were told to form a Protection Committee, so that they might work out which of their rooms could be used.

The size of the refuge room was also important. Planning for gas attacks as if they were very likely, the government informed householders of the number of people that could survive in an airtight space for twelve hours before the oxygen would run out. A room of around 10 feet squared could hold five people; one of 15 x 10, seven people; and one of 20 x 12, twelve people. It was advised that items such as candles, clean cloths, scissors, tape and a first-aid kit be kept in the room in preparation. Those who took the reinforcement of their home seriously might choose to add extra support to the ceiling of a room by building in wooden props from the floor to the ceiling, to make a cave-in less likely.

To make the room sufficiently airtight, any cracks in walls or around windows had to be fixed. To do this, it was suggested that old newspaper be pasted over the holes to seal them – not an especially pretty decorative addition, but a necessary one. Even the keyholes of doors had to be sealed. A blanket would then be nailed to the door frame, fastened to the wood on the top and at one side, to keep out gas.

To prevent windows from shattering if a bomb fell nearby, people pasted thin fabric (such as linen), paper or cellulose over the glass. Throughout the war, the now-iconic image of windows taped in a cross, or star-shaped, way was a familiar sight.

While in 1938 a refuge room was seen as the best protection one could provide at home, it actually offered little defence against high-explosive bombs. To guard against the worst of bombing, air-raid shelters were set up. People living in urban areas were most likely to use a communal shelter, which could be below ground, in cellars or tunnels, or in specially constructed buildings. In Stockport, a network of tunnels almost a mile long was used as a shelter, complete with toilets, first-aid post and electric lighting. The Cabinet War Rooms, the base of the wartime government, were constructed below the Office of Works in London, in what had previously been a storage area. Far more than just a shelter, this collection of rooms housed a map room, bedroom, typists' pool, transatlantic telephone room and Cabinet room, where meetings of the Prime Minister and his ministers and advisers took place. Broadcasting equipment allowed Winston Churchill, when Prime Minister, to deliver speeches to the nation from his underground stronghold.

Many London civilians took to sheltering in the Tube stations, which was initially discouraged for reasons of safety and hygiene; toilet facilities were not seen to be suitable in many places. Later in the war, it became apparent that there was no resisting the masses, who continued to shelter regardless of the rules. In September 1940, the government performed a tactical about-face and set about improving facilities so that the underground stations could be used as official shelters. Despite this, they were by no means a guarantee of safety. In 1940, sixty-eight people were killed in Balham Tube station when a bomb struck overhead, destroying the water mains and sewage pipes. Three years later, 173 people were crushed to death at Bethnal Green Tube station when the crowd panicked after hearing an explosion.

Many factories had basements that were used as shelters for employees; however, this posed the alternative danger of being located under several tons of machinery when bombs were falling and buildings were weakened.

People living in more rural areas – or at least, those with gardens – often opted for an Anderson shelter. Made of galvanised steel panels that could be fixed together, this was erected outside and partly buried in the ground. The introduction of shelters such as these had been discussed in the newspapers as early as November 1938, when air-raid precautions in the event of war were discussed in the House of Commons. The ideal, it was decided, was that every person in the country should have access to blast-proof accommodation. At this point, it was estimated that up to 500,000 paid ARP workers would be needed during wartime. The Anderson shelter, named after Sir John Anderson, the Minister for Civilian Defence and Lord Privy Seal, was exhibited by the Wandsworth Borough Council in April 1939, five months before the outbreak of war, as part of a National Service display in Hyde Park. The display also featured first-aid demonstrations and an exhibition of new weapons. The shelter had first become available to the public in February 1939. It was issued free of charge to households earning £250 or less each year, and at a cost of £7 to those who earned above this.

While the Anderson shelter was a good idea on paper – it absorbed a great deal of the shock from blasts without falling apart and provided good cover from falling debris – it was not a particularly attractive proposition. The shelters often flooded, and had to be equipped with pumps to remove rain water. They were also cold and often cramped – each shelter could contain six occupants but didn't take up a great deal of ground room. Households would receive their shelter as separate steel panels, and were required to do the digging and assembling themselves. Firstly, a pit around 4 feet deep had to be dug, with the shelter then being built inside it. The steel panels, curved for the roof and straight for the sides, bolted together with a cut-out hole for a door. Constructing this, including the digging, was not an easy job and some neighbours chose to work together to help each other get their shelters up.

'The Anderson' did not arrive with any beds or comforts, and conditions inside were dictated by the amount of effort each family put into them. Some opted for bunk beds as a way of housing more people in relative comfort. Nonetheless, on waking to hear an air-raid siren in the middle of the night, it must have been frightening and unpleasant to run into the garden in total darkness – no outside lights or torches allowed – to sit in a wet and unheated shelter with bombs falling overhead.

If you lived in a city or didn't have a garden, from 1941 one alternative to these cold or communal spaces was the Morrison shelter. Named after the Minister of Home Security, Herbert Morrison (later Home Secretary), this was essentially a reinforced steel cage with a solid top and cage sides. This structure would be placed inside the home, but being such a large item, the shelter took up a lot of room and was also used as a table. The main advantage to this was that when the air raid siren sounded – as it did on a very regular basis during heavy bombing periods – there was no need to go outside and leave the warmth of the home. Blankets and provisions could be kept beneath the shelter so that a certain degree of comfort was achieved. If a bomb should strike nearby, the strong shelter roof would protect its inhabitants from falling debris. It was designed to withstand the weight of an upper floor of the house collapsing. Those whose combined household income was less than £350 a year qualified for a free Morrison shelter. If you earned above this and had to buy one, it would cost (in April 1941) £7 12s 6d. The shelter would arrive in panels, and it was left to the recipient to assemble the finished article. When it was first introduced, the Morrison shelter was available only in certain areas and those wishing to obtain one were required to make an application to their local authority. For some families, the shelter certainly proved its worth. In 1942, one Exeter family's home received a direct hit, which flung the indoor shelter outside and into another house. Remarkably, none of the occupants were killed; one child escaped unharmed, while an adult and child suffered some injuries.

Entertainment

On 1 September, the television service, only used by a small minority across Britain, was suspended for the war, and local radio programming also followed suit. It was feared that the enemy might use television and regional radio as a means of navigation around

Britain. Instead, the national 'Home Service' radio was introduced, broadcast from London. For the following six years, this became an essential part of everyday life for those living on the home front – the service was the fastest and most effective way to keep up to date with news, and to receive government updates and advice on rationing and domestic concerns. One early-morning programme dictated physical exercises, a precursor to the modern-day fitness DVD. Exercises for men and women were broadcast on alternate days.

In addition to the British Home Service, listeners at home could tune in to foreign channels, including broadcasts from Germany. The Nazi Party was perhaps one of the most proficient users of propaganda, and utilised it to great effect, including through radio channels aimed at their enemies. Most famous, listened to by great numbers of people, were the broadcasts of 'Lord Haw-Haw'. The moniker originally referred to several English-speaking broadcasters within Germany, who as a team spoke of British failure and high Allied casualties in an attempt to demoralise the public. The name Lord Haw-Haw gradually came to refer exclusively to William Joyce, a fascist of Irish descent, born in America but afterwards living in Germany, who was responsible for most broadcasts from 1939 onwards. Listeners in Britain came to despise Joyce and his distinctive nasal welcome: "This is Germany calling, Germany calling." Though they knew that the programming was Nazi propaganda, high numbers tuned in in the hope of gleaning some small nuggets of truth about loved ones overseas.

Broadcasting news in English afforded the Germans an opportunity to refute claims made by the British and argue against Allied propaganda. On the day that war broke out, radio stations criticised the British and Polish for their aggression towards Germany, a country which really wanted peace. In 1940, Joyce broadcast to disagree with rumours of British and French origin that Germany intended to create panic in the Balkans, which had so far been kept out of the war. He argued that 'every German interest favours the maintenance of peace in the Balkans, whereas only England and France could be interested in causing trouble in this region'.

Joyce also criticised Winston Churchill on several occasions, including in February 1940, when he pointed out that Churchill had congratulated the captain of the HMS *Cossack* for his gallant rescue of prisoners aboard a German ship, despite the fact that the captain had, he argued, shot unarmed men and violated Norwegian neutrality. Not only did Joyce's broadcasts sometimes unsettle the British certainty that 'good' would eventually triumph over 'evil', but they also, on occasions such as this, attempted to make listeners question whether their perception of who was good was actually correct.

After the war, Joyce was tried for treason – though he had become a naturalised German subject – and hanged on 3 January 1946 at Wandsworth Prison. The main reason that prosecutors were able to find Joyce guilty was his possession of a British passport despite him technically being an American citizen. A case was made that the passport meant that at the time of his broadcasts he considered himself a British subject and so committed treason. Had he not acquired it, his life may well have been saved. Joyce was one of very few people of the time to be hanged in Britain for a crime other than murder.

The 'Phoney War'

Despite immediate precautions such as gas masks, air-raid shelters and the blackout, to those at home it seemed that very little actually happened at the beginning of the war. In fact, this early phase became known as the 'Phoney War', with no major events taking place. Some termed it the 'Bore War', while Winston Churchill preferred 'Twilight War'. The declaration of war by France and Britain was a step towards honouring a promise to assist Poland in its time of need, but beyond this there was no attempt to mount serious military action. France seemed to take up a position of defence, rather than attack, while the British were wary of bombing Germany for fear of retaliatory air raids. British and French troops guarded the Maginot Line dividing France from Germany, while most of the German army was in Poland. The main arena of action for Allied forces was the sea; the Battle of the Atlantic began in September 1939 with Nazi destroyers and U-boats targeting British and French shipping.

As little seemed to be happening, small hopes for peace grew and people debated whether it would 'all be over by Christmas'.

The Blackout

The blackout procedure was implemented on 1 September, 1939, two days before war was announced. Householders were not permitted to allow any light to escape from doors and windows, street lighting was switched off and even the glow from a cigarette outdoors was prohibited. Thick material was placed over windows, or tightly fitting canvas and wood frames were put together. The first time the blackout fell, it was as if a literal dark cloud had crossed over the people of Britain, matching the fear and dread that most felt at the prospect of war. Any glimmer of light was blotted out from the landscape and the nation was left alone in darkness.

Heavy fines and public scorn could fall on those careless enough to show a light during the blackout. The blackout was in place from dawn to dusk every night, whether air raids were predicted or not. Preserving the darkness was taken very seriously, and those who allowed light to be seen could be accused of helping to bring the Luftwaffe over a town. Those who were found to show light could be summoned to a magistrate's court and fined around £15.

Some people living in rural areas that were unlikely to be targeted for bombing complained that blackout restrictions were unnecessary and too severe. However, there were several very sensible reasons put forward for the unpopular rules. Though insignificant in size, rural communities were often located near to important military sites that could be targeted. Another fear was that, despite their smallness, rural villages that were lit would show up so obviously alongside blacked-out towns and cities that they could become easy targets for bombers. Finally, it was argued that the visible rural areas surrounding a large pool of darkness that was a city would indicate very clearly that it was there, making blackout restrictions in these built-up areas worthless. Despite much grumbling, the blackout was upheld with all possible vigour.

Perhaps not surprisingly, many accidents occurred due to the dangerously dark conditions. In early September, only days after the blackout's introduction, newspapers reported the tale of an elderly woman who had been run over and killed by a car. Following this, pedestrians were advised to pause outside on the pavement after leaving a brightly lit building, to allow their eyes to better adjust and to consider wearing light clothing, carrying a newspaper or wearing a white armband. One coroner, after presiding over the inquests of twelve people killed in the blackout in September alone, advised that elderly people 'who had no business or occasion to be on the street' should stay at home during the evening 'and not embarrass those whose duty it is to drive vehicles at night'. He stated that of the twelve fatal cases he had seen eight had been over the age of sixty-eight. The total number of road deaths during September alone, while including those that were non-blackout-related, was extremely high at 1,130. Eventually, small torches were permitted in an attempt to keep casualty numbers down.

Some also turned the blackout to their advantage. One man was sentenced to five years in prison in September 1939 for burglary of a house during a blackout, and in Regent Street £3,000 worth of furs was stolen.

When the clocks changed to mark the end of British Summer Time, these problems became worse still, as the period of darkness each evening grew longer. One solution put forward, and eventually adopted, was to extend British Summer Time for the duration of the war.

Month One

Day 1

Before the first day of my experiment has even begun, the loss of modern life has begun to impact. Last night I dreamt of television, waking up to feel slightly confused before remembering that today is 3 September 1939. Though excited, I feel a little thrown out of my comfort zone. While normally I might watch something online while I eat my breakfast, I sat by a window in the sun and began *The Murder of Roger Ackroyd* by Agatha Christie. Not at all unpleasant, just a change to a well-formed routine.

Today's outfit is a bit of a shocker; I haven't quite got the hang of dressing for 1939 yet. My trousers are perfectly fine – luckily for me, the 1940s style has come back into fashion, so I have on a fairly new pair of grey, woollen high-waisted trousers. With these are an old white cotton blouse left over from my secondary school days, and a blue cardigan that by all logic should match well enough but doesn't seem to. While I might not be the best-looking member of the home front, I am very comfortable; more so than in my usual jeans and t-shirt. I wonder why this is. The only conclusion I can come to is that my clothes might normally be tighter than this, or that the materials might somehow have less 'give'?

For lunch, I decided to make the most of unlimited cheese (the rationed amount doesn't give me much to hope for) and make cheese scones. These are delicious, and I don't know why I don't make them more often. I think convenience food is far too convenient, as although I love cooking I don't bother with things like scones and bread very often.

For dinner this evening, Benjamin and I had steak with beef-dripping-roasted potatoes and salad. Banished are the oven chips that would usually accompany such a meal – just as such humorously large steaks will soon be banished by the meat ration. Still, it's lovely while it lasts. Especially when washed down with some of last summer's home-brewed wine and accompanied by an after-dinner win at Monopoly. So far, the television switch-off hasn't hit home.

Day 2

As I had hoped, I seem to be getting more work done now that I am living in 1939. Working from home is always tricky, with a multitude of distractions to ensure that a day is successfully wasted. However, without the lure of television and pointless websites, it is slightly easier to stay on task. The only distraction calling me now is *The Murder of Roger Ackroyd*, which will invariably receive some attention.

This evening, my sister Lauren and I went to see family – usually, one night a week is dedicated to a family takeaway and film. I was a bit apprehensive before going, as I worry that others are not as keen as me on giving the Second World War leisure pursuits a try; particularly at the expense of television. Just in case, I took a book with me to read, should I become outvoted and have to excuse myself from the room. Sure enough, there were some grumbles about missing a certain television programme, but eventually we settled on a game of Scrabble. Dinner was easy to resolve, as fish and chips were available in the late 1930s and seem to please everyone. After Scrabble, and a wondrous victory on my part, we settled down to a fast-paced quiz game. By the time it came for us to leave, everyone was in a thoroughly good mood and planning what we could do next week. Success!

Day 3

I've already finished reading my Agatha Christie novel, which is both surprising and quite satisfying at the same time. The weather for the last two days has been awful, quashing all plans for midday walks and vegetable-patch preparation. But somehow, it seems like time is better spent reading a book than watching a television programme. They're both just forms of entertainment, but a book feels more enriching – if that makes sense.

Having said that, one of my favourite television series began on the BBC this evening, much to my disappointment. It's something that I normally look forward to. There was some discussion of cheating and watching it, but I think I'd feel a bit like I'd let myself down if I gave in so early on in the year. So it came and went unwatched, and in a fit of grumpiness I was generally quite rotten. In hindsight, this seems ridiculous, but the change in evening routine has started to get a bit more challenging. I didn't realise I'd miss television this much, this soon.

Day 4

I need to set about sorting out my blackout, but have no idea where to begin. I wish I'd accosted Benjamin and asked him to help me. In the spirit of those women who took on so much while their husbands were away, I shall sort it out myself! But what to use? Will an old towel suffice? I suspect not.

However, there is now masking tape in the distinctive cross shape over my windows. This is strangely oppressive and suddenly makes the war feel rather real. Whenever I catch it out of the corner of my eye, I am momentarily startled by the change.

Day 6

Another very successful day in terms of work. I've got more done this week than in every week before the war, which encourages me.

This evening, Lauren watched the television so I retreated upstairs to listen to Noel Coward and read the newspapers from September

1939. Though obviously there's much discussion of the war, very little of note seems to be happening. I was expecting exciting developments and far more propaganda; perhaps this is the same sense of anti-climax that led people to declare this period the 'Phoney War'? It seems wrong, but in a cruel way I'm looking forward to the beginning of the Blitz, when there'll be far more to read about. I know that if this were real, I would be dreading such a thing. The papers contain a large amount of conjecture over what the effect of bombing could be, but as yet it was hard for civilians to know what to expect. My research tells me that the consequences of bombing, when the Blitz did begin, were nowhere near as bad as people imagined. In hospitals, 750,000 beds were made ready for air-raid victims, though only around 6,000 were actually required.

The most dramatic thing to have happened so far is the famous Coventry murders of August 1939. Elsie Ansell, Rex Gentle, John Corbett Arnott, Gwilym Rowlands and James Clay had the misfortune to become caught in a fierce terrorist explosion plotted by the IRA. A bicycle was bought for the crime, and a bomb hidden in a brown paper parcel was placed in its basket. Around 1.45 p.m., the bicycle was left outside a shop called Astley's where it exploded. The crime, though tragic, was overshadowed by the declaration of war soon after. Reading a newspaper from 5 October reveals that five people – husband and wife Joseph and Mary Hewitt; Mary Hewitt's mother, Brigid O'Hara; James Richards and Peter Barnes – were charged with the murder of Elsie Ansell, and on 6 October committed for trial.

The trial played out over four days from 11 December. Two of the five defendants, James Richards and Peter Barnes, were found guilty and sentenced to death. The Hewitts and Brigid O'Hara were acquitted, though they later stood trial over the death of the four other victims. Little evidence for the prosecution could be found, and in each case they were found not guilty.

Day 10

After putting it off for as long as possible, today I finally gave in and did some of my washing. This was a task even more tedious and lengthy than I had feared. My fingers pruned, my hands went red and I became more than a little cranky. Despite scrubbing and scrubbing, I have been forced to accept that one particularly dirty pair of pale blue socks is probably never going to be clean again; not until I return to the modern day, that is. Everything is made harder by the fact that I don't have any of the items at the disposal of a 1930s housewife, such as a scrubbing board or mangle. I'm not sure about my chances of getting hold of either of those items in the modern day; not on my tight budget. I might keep a look-out, however; a mangle would be so useful. At the moment, my clothes are drip-drying at a snail's pace.

I am absolutely dreading having to wash my bedding – it doesn't even bear thinking about. No wonder housewives used to dedicate a whole day to washing. Nowadays – placing washing in the washing machine, adding powder and pressing the 'start' button – it is so much easier. I think I have taken that for granted so far.

Day 12

Today I went shopping with my mother, sister and grandmother. Ordinarily, I would want and expect to spend money on things like clothes, and feel a bit disappointed if I didn't. It was quite liberating, for a change, to know that I didn't really need to do this. I don't need many new clothes, except a cardigan (which I bought), and the wartime lifestyle doesn't lend itself as well to frivolous purchases. I went with one main aim – to have a nice cup of tea out and to buy some wool for knitting. Both missions accomplished, I was perfectly happy; and left with far more money than usual.

The wool for knitting is dark blue, and will be made into a scarf for my grandfather. He's difficult to buy for on birthdays and at Christmas, so I'm hoping that the fact I've made him something will make the present more special. An added bonus is that it is less pricey, and more meaningful, to make a present than it is to simply walk into a shop and buy something.

This evening (being Saturday night) Ben and I had an 'old movie night' and watched *The Bride of Frankenstein* (1935), starring Boris Karloff. It was lovely to settle down with a film again, and I enjoyed it even more than I thought I would. It was far better than the original *Frankenstein*, though the monster's bride didn't feature as heavily as I had expected. It's strange to watch things that don't have the polish and special effects that we are used to today, but this didn't seem to make it any less enjoyable.

Day 13

An extremely productive Sunday. Usually this day marks a concerted effort at a 'day of rest', incorporating TV marathons and a spot of leisurely baking. Today, however, Ben and I got to work early, me pruning the hydrangeas and clearing more space for vegetables in the borders (now less ornamental) while Ben attempted to see if a partially rotten piece of trellis could be salvaged for further use; it could! Some sawing, painting and one cut thumb later, something that I had consigned to the rubbish heap was as good as new and ready to be affixed to the wall for morning glory plants and peas to trail up. The next problem was the wall itself.

The back of our house hasn't been painted for years, and we were both reluctant to put the 'new' trellis on such a green mess. Out came the paintbrushes and a tin of half-empty white paint – in no time, the house was looking far better and we were rewarding ourselves with sausage sandwiches. I appreciated the sausages – there may be no more of those once the meat ration comes in.

My 'victory garden' is beginning to shape up now – a little more clearance work is still needed before it's ready for the first crops, but there should eventually be a fairly sizeable space.

Day 16

This evening, tempted a little too soon by the prospect of an old film, we watched Alfred Hitchcock's *The 39 Steps*. Despite the fact that it is over 75 years old, it has to be one of the best films I've seen in a long time. The suspense was every bit as fresh as it must have been in the 1930s cinema, and the two lead characters (Robert Donat and Madeleine Carroll) played off each other brilliantly. It's hard to believe that it's as old as it is. The theme of spies and foreign conflict is present, even though this was released four years before the outbreak of war. Perhaps I'm reading too much into it, but I wonder how early tensions were really apparent to the general public, even then?

Day 18

Reading through newspaper reports of German atrocities in Poland, it dawned on me how terrifying this must have been for those living on the home front. I can sit comfortably knowing that the Germans never invaded Britain, but my Second World War counterparts must have considered this a real possibility. Hearing how the Nazis rounded up inhabitants of a Polish village at random and shot them, they must have feared the day when they could be in the same situation. It suddenly makes the war seem a bit more real. Invasion was not beyond the realms of possibility – by December 1939, Finland and Poland had both been invaded, Finland being taken by Russia. I wonder what on earth would have happened if we in Britain had faced the reality of invasion.

Tonight, Ben and my friends Becky and Aaron came over and the four of us played Monopoly (first introduced in the UK in 1935, if anyone's wondering). What ensued was a thoroughly enjoyable (if competitive) evening, without the interruption of television. Interestingly, in 1941 the British Secret Service used Monopoly very much to its advantage. Games company Waddingtons produced a special version that was sent to prisoners of war, concealing real money, maps and compasses to help them escape.

Day 20

In addition to my garden vegetable beds, I also have the option of extending my 'Dig for Victory' campaign to Ben's allotment. This isn't as convenient in terms of location, as it is further away and therefore the crops aren't quite 'to hand' in the same way. However, there is far more space, and there are several large empty beds that can be put to good use.

Today was dedicated to working on the allotment – clearing the area of weeds and digging over the beds to start preparing the soil. Ben's parents (in the allotment next door) also had several fruit canes that had been forgotten about, which we were allowed to move into our space and replant.

Turning over the beds was fairly hard work, as they've been neglected somewhat during the winter. It was also a cold day, with wet ground from a morning downpour. In all, the experience was probably fairly similar to that shared by the Diggers for Victory of October 1939. One perk is that the allotment also has a shed, perfect for sheltering from the cold wind with a flask.

It's still a little too early to plant most produce, but we did manage to sow some carrot and pickling onion seeds.

Day 24

My hands are starting to suffer from the wartime way of life – hand washing and increased gardening have made them dry and cracked around the cuticles. After a particularly vigorous bout of cleaning this morning, I now have blisters on my right hand and a bleeding cuticle.

An American 1942 advert (a little ahead of my time, but close enough) for Pacquin's hand cream is aimed at female war workers, telling the tale of a factory worker whose rough hands cause her discomfort and embarrassment.

I shall have to look for a good home solution to the problem.

Recipe Card: Leftover Chicken Pie

This is very much a pre-rationing recipe; it's unlikely that a household would get hold of a whole chicken during meat rationing. The amount of chicken included depends entirely on how much you have available; if you have less chicken, add more mushrooms.

Ingredients:

3 oz/85 g butter
Leftover chicken – enough to half-fill a pie dish
6 oz/170 g mushrooms
1 onion
2 tbsp plain flour
Approx. ½ pint milk
150 ml chicken stock
Chopped fresh parsley
8 oz/225 g shortcrust pastry (made with 8 oz flour and 4 oz/115 g butter)
Salt and pepper to taste
1 egg or a small drop of milk to glaze

Method:

If you want to make a really authentic pie, it's best to make the most of the chicken and make your own stock. This has the added benefit of using as much of the bird as possible, eliminating waste.

Strip the leftover chicken from the chicken carcass and set aside in the fridge (or larder) for later. Place the carcass in a large pan, add water to almost cover it, bring it to the boil and simmer for around 2–3 hours. The length of time can be adjusted to suit however long you have available, but the longer the cooking the more concentrated your stock will be. When this is ready, take out the carcass and strip off any more chicken that has been loosened before discarding. Pour the pan of stock through a sieve to fish out any rogue bones that might remain. If you don't have the time to make stock, simply use a chicken stock cube later on in the recipe.

To make the pie, firstly chop the leftover chicken into manageable lumps. Fry the mushrooms and onion in 1 oz/25 g of butter until golden, adding the chopped chicken at the end for around a minute. Place these together in the pie dish.

The next step is to make a white sauce – different people have different preferences as to how they do this. Feel free to adjust this recipe to suit your own style, if preferred.

Melt the remaining 2 oz butter in a saucepan and add the flour, stirring constantly to make a roux (paste). Allow this to cook for around two minutes. Gradually pour the milk and stock onto the roux, vigorously stirring or whisking to avoid lumps. If lumps form, simply whisk or sieve the mixture – it happens to us all.

Simmer until the sauce has thickened to 'pie consistency' and pour into the pie dish with the chicken, onion and mushrooms.

Add the chopped parsley, stir in and season with salt and pepper according to taste. As women (and men, too) were advised in wartime recipes, don't be stingy with seasoning!

Roll out your pastry (homemade or shop-bought) so that it will fit over the pie dish. Brush the edges of the dish with milk, cut a thin strip of pastry and stick it – using the milk – around the edge of the dish, forming a lip that your pie lid can be fixed to. Brush the pastry rim with milk (not too much, or the whole thing will slide around) and place the rolled-out pastry on top. Cut around the edge of the dish with a knife so that the pastry fits neatly and press down around the edges to fasten.

Glaze the pie with more milk (or egg, if you prefer), pierce with a knife and cook in the oven at 200°C/Gas Mark 6 for around thirty minutes until the pastry looks cooked and golden.

In the Kitchen Garden

Things to Do:
February
Sow seeds indoors or under cover (e.g. in a greenhouse, cold frame or under cloches) for celery, summer cauliflower and early summer cabbages such as Greyhound. Herbs such as rosemary, basil and sage can also be sown indoors now. Garlic can be planted directly into the ground.

CHAPTER TWO: 1940

The Perils of Rationing (March–April)

In 1940

8 January: Food rationing is introduced, with limits set on quantities of sugar, butter, bacon and/or ham. Butter and bacon and ham are each rationed to 4 oz per person per week, while sugar is restricted to 12 oz per person.

11 February: Russia's Red Army launches a fierce military campaign against Finland.

11 March: The meat ration is introduced. Each person is allowed meat to the value of 1s 10d each week.

3 April: Lord Woolton is appointed Minister of Food. He would later give his name to the infamous Woolton Pie.

8 April: Hitler's forces invade Denmark and Norway.

10 May: Neville Chamberlain stands down as Prime Minister, and Winston Churchill takes his place as the head of a new coalition government. The Germans launch 'Blitzkrieg', a concentrated attack, against Holland, Belgium, Luxembourg and France.

13 May: Germany invades France. Newspapers report that parts of the country have been bombed, and peasants working in a field machine-gunned.

14 May: The Secretary of State for War calls for more Local Defence Volunteers, men between the ages of seventeen and sixty-five, to guard against possible German parachute landings in Britain. The Netherlands surrenders to the German forces.

27 May: Sugar ration reduced from 12 oz to 8 oz.

28 May: Belgium's King Leopold surrenders.

4 June: 'Operation Dynamo', the Admiralty's mission to rescue troops from Dunkirk, concludes with a total of 338,000 evacuated. In the House of Commons, Churchill makes his famous 'we shall fight them on the beaches' speech. In other news, it is reported that on instructions from the Ministry of Transport all signposts in Britain have now been painted out, so that German invaders cannot navigate using them.

9 June: The Germans achieve control of Norway.

18 June: In a speech to the Commons, Churchill declares that 'the battle of France is over. I expect that the battle of Britain is about to begin.'

30 June: German troops land on the Channel Islands, beginning five years of Nazi occupation.

3 July: Cardiff is bombed.

9 July: Tea is rationed to 2 oz per person per week and is price controlled.

15 July: From this date, eating out at restaurants changes slightly. Only one course of meat, game, poultry or fish may be served

to each person at a meal. Meals such as this do not fall under rationing, however, and can be enjoyed without coupons.

19 July: In an address to the Reichstag, Hitler appeals to the UK for peace. The British Foreign Minister, Lord Halifax, rejects Germany's peace conditions.

22 July: Margarine and cooking fats are included in rationing. Each person now has one 'butter and margarine' coupon, with which they may buy a total weekly amount of 6 oz butter and/or margarine, and one 'cooking fats' coupon, with which they may buy a further 2 oz cooking fats, including margarine and lard.

9 August: Birmingham is heavily bombed.

22 August: Germany prepares to launch 'Operation Sea Lion', the invasion of Britain.

24 August: Central London is bombed for the first time. Casualties are relatively few, though many fires are caused.

25 August: The RAF bombs Berlin.

7 September: London suffers the first of seventy-six consecutive nights of bombing – the Blitz.

13 September: During a daylight raid, Buckingham Palace is bombed for the second time in one week, destroying the Chapel Royal. The king and queen are in residence but appear unshaken and unscathed. The queen later comments, 'I am glad we have been bombed. It makes me feel that I can look the East End in the face.'

17 September: Hitler decides to postpone the invasion of Britain after defeat in the Battle of Britain. For 'Operation Sea Lion' to have succeeded, the Germans would have needed air and naval supremacy over the English Channel, something the Battle of Britain

had denied them. In the Atlantic, the SS *City of Benares*, a ship carrying 100 evacuees to Canada, is torpedoed causing the death of 87 children and 175 adults.

27 September: In Berlin, representatives from Japan and Italy sign the Tripartite Pact, or Axis Pact, with Germany. The pact ensures that the three nations will support each other during forthcoming conflict.

13 October: Princess Elizabeth makes her radio debut in a broadcast addressing evacuees at home and abroad.

14 November: Coventry is heavily bombed and much damaged. The centre of the city is subject to attack by 515 Luftwaffe bombers, 150,000 fire bombs and over 500 tons of explosives. 60,000 buildings are destroyed, 600 people are killed and over 1,000 injured. Hereafter, the German army will use the phrase 'to coventrate' when speaking of intense destruction.

16 December: For one week, to celebrate Christmas, the sugar ration is increased from 8 oz to 12 oz and the tea ration increased from 2 oz to 4 oz.

29 December: The City of London is heavily attacked by incendiary bombs and high-explosive bombs, causing such extensive damage by fire that it is named the Second Great Fire of London. Eight historic churches designed by Christopher Wren are destroyed, in addition to many other important and commercial buildings.

In January 1940, four months after the outbreak of war, rationing was introduced. This was not an entirely new concept: rationing had also been put into place during the First World War. Rationing was a topic that divided opinion across Britain. Some were, naturally, opposed to the idea; in fact, the system was delayed until 1940 because of a campaign against it that was run in the *Daily Mail*. Others – most likely the majority of people – were in favour of rationing as it ensured that everybody received a guaranteed amount of food each week, rather than risking the possibility of class bias through rising prices or an outright lack of food.

Rationing was, in times of war, a foregone conclusion. By the beginning of the twentieth century, Britain was importing vast amounts of its food and had long given up on self-sufficiency. During peacetime, a system of imports and exports worked well for the nation and its economy, but during hostilities the country was left in a vulnerable position. German forces attacked supply ships and importing became difficult and deadly. The population was taught to hate waste, as many lives were lost while shipping food. Cartoons with cautionary lines appeared in newspapers to reinforce the message: 'Night and day men of the Royal Navy cheerfully risk their lives to guard your food. They don't mind danger but waste gives them the creeps!'

Not only was food importing from Allied countries difficult, but the number of countries able to supply Britain also diminished. During 1940, several previous suppliers, such as Denmark, Belgium, France and Holland, fell to the Nazis and were no longer able to export. Holland, for instance, had previously supplied the country with large quantities of eggs and vegetables. For these reasons, the Dig for Victory campaign became absolutely essential as an additional source of food.

Rationing was introduced slowly but surely, beginning with foods that were perceived to be initially in short supply. Sugar, bacon, ham and butter came first on 8 January, followed by meat in March and tea and cooking fats in July. Other items that are now thought of as traditionally rationed, such as eggs and sweets, were not restricted until later in the war. Before a food became rationed, there was sometimes a period of time in which it was very hard to get hold of. When cheese was put on the ration, most people were relieved as the even distribution meant that they were able to get more of it than they had before.

Many foods were restricted in ways other than rationing. During 1940, the varieties of bread that could be made were reduced; instead of forty-five different shapes and sizes being commonly manufactured by bakers, the available range was limited to four types. Confectioners and bakers were told that they were now forbidden from using icing on cakes.

In some villages, encouraged by the Ministry of Agriculture, pig clubs were formed. This was seen as a positive way of utilising household food scraps, such as vegetable peelings, as they could be fed to a pig in order to fatten it for eating. Clubs were formed by organisations such as the Women's Institute, Young Farmers and parish councils, and involved several participants sharing a pig.

Rationing was taken very seriously indeed and was enforceable by law. In May 1940, a woman was fined £2 with one guinea costs for obtaining meat over the rationed amount, while the butcher that supplied her was forced to pay a fine of £20 with two guineas costs. Shopkeepers could also be fined for supplying goods without taking coupons; the same butcher also received a further fine of £20 for 'selling without coupons'.

Fruit was not rationed but was simply not available for most of the time. From mid-1940, the government announced that it would no longer be importing fruit, save for a limited number of oranges for children only. Members of the public who became concerned about missing out on vitamin C were advised to eat greater quantities of broccoli, spinach, turnip tops and swede. Food was blander, with less variety, but ultimately as healthy (if not healthier) if ministry-issued advice was followed.

In fact, nutrition was given a strong focus during the Second World War. When the Ministry of Food was established, top nutritionists were employed to look closely at the nation's needs. An ideal diet was 'sold' to the public, in which four food groups were identified:

1 Body-building foods, including meat, fish, cheese and eggs.
2 Energy foods, including bacon and ham, bread, cooking fats, cheese, dried fruit and potatoes.
3 Protective foods (1), including milk, butter, liver, eggs and herrings.
4 Protective foods (2), including potatoes, carrots, fruit, green vegetables and wholemeal bread.

This diet was nutritionally sensible but also conveniently comprised the foods that were available at the time. When potatoes were in abundance, propaganda would extol their health benefits. The now well-known characters of Potato Pete and Dr Carrot were created to encourage people to eat healthily and grow their own vegetables. More was published on the benefits of different vitamins, and in which foods they could be found.

Food rationing saw the beginning of a new style of cookery. Many wartime recipes such as Woolton Pie are now well-known, while others have been considered better forgotten. Housewives became extremely inventive, creating meals out of a limited number of ingredients. Dishes were given optimistic or mysterious names to disguise their ingredients: mock apricot flan made with carrots, mock crab made with dried egg and cheese, mock goose made with apples, and Victory Sponge, a dessert made with potato and carrot. Most had nothing whatsoever to do with their names; mock crab, for instance, would taste nothing like crab.

In April 1940, the 'Kitchen Front' campaign was launched by the recently appointed Minister of Food, Lord Woolton. The Kitchen Front was targeted at women and encouraged economy in the use of food with the aim of reducing the number of food imports needed. Though sexist by modern standards, the Kitchen Front was seen as a major way in which women could contribute to the war effort.

On 5 April Woolton declared,

To-day, in my first speech as Minister of Food, I am going to tell them. I am going to venture at the outset of my work to call on the women of England to mobilise themselves on the Kitchen Front. It doesn't sound romantic; it doesn't sound grand; it isn't dangerous work – but it is vital to our victory. I want the women of England to go into training for the days which may come when the whole staying power of the nation will depend on them ... I want them to consider how to do without things and how to use the food we have to the best advantage.

Lord Woolton was supported by the wife of Prime Minister Neville Chamberlain, who agreed that she and other housewives needed guidance on the best use of food in wartime. By approaching the matter with 'the right spirit', she claimed women could find problems with food to be interesting and ultimately beneficial to their cooking skills. Every morning at 8.15 a.m., a five-minute Kitchen Front radio broadcast shared food ideas, recipes and news. Cookery demonstrations were also held locally, to give every woman the best possible chance of success. These demonstrations covered a number of basic topics, such as different ways to serve vegetables and 'new ways of preparing salads'. Newspapers carried regular Kitchen Front messages entitled Food Facts, containing seasonal advice, waste-saving tips and encouraging words: 'Every time you cook you can help or hinder Hitler!' As the year went on and bombing began, these messages began to reflect the tension felt by the public. Instead of recipes for jam, the instalments carried guidelines on how to protect food from bomb dust and glass splinters.

Helping out at Home

Volunteering and community involvement grew dramatically during 1940. The year before, the government had appealed for more volunteers across many different sectors. Aiming to build up a reserve of 700,000 part-time Air Raid Precautions (ARP) wardens, the Home Office promised compensation for loss of earnings to those who would help. This compensation, up to the value of ten shillings a week for men and seven shillings a week for women, was paid by the local authorities, who were then reimbursed by the government. ARP wardens were responsible for assessing bomb damage and patrolling the streets during blackouts to ensure that no light could be seen from houses and workplaces. Though these men and women were unpopular, theirs was seen as a vital role. As early as 1935, Britain had been alerted to the need for air-raid shelters in the event of war. Attack from the skies was greatly feared, and any step to lessen possible damage and death was naturally encouraged.

By 1940, civilians were offering their services for all kinds of voluntary war work. Many took on extra duties in addition to full-time jobs. Fire watching was a common practice and a real community effort: groups of volunteers would take up nightly posts on the tops of buildings or inside houses with a good vantage point of the local area. Their role was to watch for, and sometimes extinguish, incendiary bombs. These bombs, though not as dramatically dangerous as high explosives, were nonetheless extremely destructive and generally nasty to deal with. They had first been used during attack on Britain in 1915, during the First World War. A large outer casing was filled with several smaller fire bombs, generally packed with combustible chemicals such as phosphorous or magnesium. This outside shell would open in the air, scattering the smaller bombs on the ground below to hit a wider target area. The bombs began raging fires which ripped through buildings. If the fires could be attended to quickly, the lives of many could be saved. Fire watchers, observing a bomb fall, were able to call through to the authorities and alert them to the fact. They were also equipped with stirrup pumps and buckets of sand and water so that bombs falling nearby could be extinguished. Theirs was a vital role; without volunteers, there wouldn't have been the sheer manpower to watch over such a large proportion of Britain. In September 1940, fire watching was made compulsory for some men under the Fire Watchers Order, though many people continued to carry out the service voluntarily. At this time, the government issued an order under the Defence Regulations that a fire watcher must be present at all times in any premises in which thirty or more people worked.

A similar role to fire watching was roof spotting. This was common in industrial areas, particularly around factories. A great amount of valuable working time was lost during air raids, despite the fact that German planes were often not in the immediate area at the time. It was thought that the planes would fly around purely in order to 'set off' sirens and hinder the manufacture of materials as a workforce was made to shelter. Volunteers instead manned observation posts on the roofs of buildings after the 'alert' siren had sounded; this way, if an enemy aircraft was seen by a roof spotter, those working in the factories could be told that the warning was genuine. In such a case, the descent to an air-raid shelter had to be immediate. Though risky, roof spotting was a shrewd business move and prevented much wasted time. For those volunteering, it was a difficult and stressful job with heavy responsibility attached.

The Women's Voluntary Service (WVS) was formed in 1938 as part of the ARP plans. Launched by a woman named Stella Isaacs, Marchioness of Reading, the WVS helped to shape a very real and active way that women could be involved in war work. Members of the WVS took their places on the front line of the war at home, attending recently bombed areas to provide immediate aid, emergency rest centres and food and drink. A uniform was designed by the London couturier Digby Morton, though volunteers had to buy it themselves and many chose not to, instead wearing a WVS badge as identification. Over the course of the war, WVS member numbers increased at an impressive rate as its women took on more duties, including salvage collection, rehoming, the evacuation of women and children and information centres for tracing missing people. The sheer amount of work carried out by these women was simply staggering – instead of being focused on one area of work alone, they consented to do anything that was needed. During the Second World War, 243 women from Britain and Northern Ireland were killed. By 1944, the WVS had 1,000,000 members, committed to doing anything and everything that needed to be done, however large or small the task.

It would be very hard for me, during the course of this experiment, to replicate the danger and urgency of this volunteering work. However, I think that it is important for accuracy that I give up more of my free time for others. To this end, I have volunteered to help out with the formation of our local history society, which is in need of people to assist with its planning and running. I have also become involved with the reopening of a local charity shop, which was recently closed down and has been saved by a rapidly formed committee of volunteers. Because of my experience working in magazines, I have taken on the role of volunteer press officer, drafting publicity material and liaising with the local media.

Britain under Fire

The Blitz has become one of the defining moments in British history – somehow memorable even in the minds of those who were not alive at the time. Since the outbreak of the Second World War, the mass-bombing of Britain had been both expected and feared. The call of the air-raid siren had rung out on a regular basis since that first day in September 1939, but it wasn't until 1940 that the distant menace became a reality. Anderson and Morrison shelters proved their worth as bombs fell for the first time and a nation took cover.

Beginning in July 1940, the initial targets for enemy attack were those integral to shipping. Portsmouth, the home of the Royal

Navy, was subjected to a fierce bombing campaign that destroyed over 6,600 residential buildings and halted the dockyard's repair of damaged Navy vessels. Though shelters were plentiful and widely used, 930 civilians were killed here during the war, and over 1,200 hospitalised.

The next tactic of the Luftwaffe was to focus energy and bombs on RAF airfields and other sites of military importance, such as aircraft factories. Many airfields, including Biggin Hill, were hit several times and in Birmingham a tyre factory was attacked.

In August 1940, the Luftwaffe bombed Croydon and Harrow, reportedly by mistake. Hitler had instructed that London was not to be bombed until he gave the command, and in a directive issued on 1 August stated that his pilots were to avoid unnecessary civilian loss of life. After these apparent attacks on London, the RAF bombed Berlin, an event that shocked and outraged Hitler and Göring, Commander-in-Chief of the Luftwaffe. Göring had not believed that Berlin would ever be directly attacked in such a way and had publicly stated as much. Hitler withdrew the directive protecting civilian lives and gave the order that the capital city was no longer off limits. Angry and embarrassed, seeking revenge, he despatched his Luftwaffe to London.

On Saturday 7 September, the city was besieged and the residential area of East London came under assault. Monday morning newspaper reports estimated that on that one day alone around 400 people were killed and between 1,300 and 1,400 injured. Defences were upheld and a reported 99 enemy planes were shot down, but the sheer size of the Luftwaffe forces made them impossible to hold back. In contrast to being a one-off event, the raids marked the first of over 70 consecutive days of attack on the city. In these early days of the Blitz, Londoners declared their spirits unbroken with a cry of 'are we downhearted? No!' Newspapers reported the RAF's successful exploits in Berlin, where military objectives such as shipyards, docks, factories and rail communications were targeted.

The bombing of Britain carried on well into the winter of 1940. It wasn't only London that suffered. In November, the city of Coventry was all but obliterated, with an estimated 80 per cent of its buildings destroyed. Codenamed 'Operation Moonlight Sonata', the Coventry attack was conducted with the aim of destroying the city's industrial infrastructure, as well as its residential and historical areas. Cities all over Britain were heavily bombed in November, with an entire street in Liverpool wrecked by one high-explosive bomb.

Airborne hostilities continued well into 1941. On 15 April 1941, Belfast saw the greatest loss of life during the Blitz outside of London. Almost a quarter of the city's population was left homeless and almost 1,000 people were killed.

Another location to be targeted was Plymouth, which was heavily bombed in the spring of 1941. On 21 April 1941, an underground air-raid shelter in the city was directly hit by a high-explosive bomb. Only two survivors emerged from a crowd of over seventy people. The historic Mount Edgcumbe house, just across the water from the city, was almost destroyed two days later when it was hit by incendiary bombs that had, in all probability, simply fallen wide of their mark.

Even rural Cornwall was not spared from bombing. Some parts of the region were legitimate targets for the enemy: the docks at Falmouth, RAF bases and airfields and anti-aircraft defences. On 21 August 1941, an RAF airfield at St Eval was targeted in a concentrated attack that destroyed a number of aircraft and injured seventeen people.

Some German planes simply took the opportunity to drop their bombs on Cornwall before heading home, in order to lighten their load. 'Terror raids' also took place – not just in Cornwall but all over Britain – with the sole aim of frightening and demoralising residents. The RAF was similarly accused of adopting the terror-bombing approach in their attacks upon Germany cities.

With the start of the Battle of Britain, the direct consequences of gunfire and explosives ceased to be contained within a distant battlefield or in foreign climes. The Blitz flew the fear of war to those living on the home front; a fear that was all too often brought vividly to life with brick-dust, rubble and fire. Houses were no longer a refuge but a target and a prison.

Remembering Coventry

Muriel Wells was a child living in Coventry at the time of the November 1940 bombing. Here, she recalls the events surrounding the devastation:

November in that year of 1940 was, as usual, dank and dark, but it had also been very wet. Our Anderson shelter in our small garden was flooded; rather inconvenient with night raids on the increase. Instead, Mum set up a temporary shelter in our tiny walk-in pantry.

On the night of the 14 November, we, having had our tea, were ensconced in this little haven because the air-raid warning had already sounded. We were snug in our siren suits, all-in-one garments that kept out the cold, and were quietly playing, with one ear on the bangs, bumps and thuds that seemed to grow nearer. I was drawing on a pad, when suddenly there was an explosion near at hand. All the lights went out, windows and doors blew in, the glass kitchen extension was shattered, and there was dust everywhere.

Mum led us down the garden path and carried my brother, Roy. Shrapnel was raining down from the anti-aircraft barrage. Dad arrived home from work and was relieved to find us all safely, if uncomfortably, installed in the Anderson shelter. However, he had to go on duty immediately, because as an ARP warden he had to deal with the many incendiaries that were dropping and later to help deal with an exploded gas main a few yards from our street. My father's beat was in the district of Paradise – but it was anything but that, that night!

The night seemed interminable and we longed for it to end. We were scared, particularly when things got close, but we knew that Mum didn't allow screaming.

Suddenly our world rocked violently and I heard three bumps followed by bangs. 'Mum do bombs bounce?' I enquired. A stick of bombs had fallen on our street. Fortune was indeed smiling upon us that night as, though our house was badly damaged and was later demolished, it still stood – in a fashion. The house next door was flattened (as was half the street), and its bedroom floor was acting as a prop to our house.

The next day, we were collected up and walked via the many detours to Webster Street, where Auntie and Gran's house was still standing, though stripped of its roof tiles. Debris and mud covered all the roads and pavements, and it became very difficult to walk and felt as though we had concrete clogs on.

Everyone helped each other in those times and often in the months ahead my sister Joyce and I shared our double bed, with three of us at the top and three at the bottom, when family or friends needed emergency accommodation.

Above all my parents made us feel safe so we never felt real fear or panic. Now I am old I can more fully appreciate their achievement, during those difficult and dangerous times.

Muriel Wells with her brother Roy and sister Joyce in the early 1940s.

Mike Fitzpatrick was also a child at the time of the Coventry bombings and remembers the disruption of the following months:
The war was pretty uneventful from September 1939 until 14 November 1940, when it all happened. My father's sister lived two doors up the road and they had built an Anderson shelter in her back garden. When the bombing started, we slept in the shelter every night and that's where we were on the night of the Blitz. While my father was away on fire-picket duty, there was a report of a German parachuting from a hit plane. My uncle did not sleep in the shelter – he was too proud and had a 'this is my house' attitude. My father was sent home from work early to check that we were safe and, as he

came through the back gate, my uncle came rushing out of the house wielding a carving knife, thinking it was the German pilot.

One of the many barrage balloons must have been damaged and came bouncing down on the roof tops, causing a lot of excitement for a while. Our house was hit pretty badly in the roof, so we could only live inside through the day. I remember sitting in the dining room with buckets on the table to catch rainwater. I also remember the bomb-disposal squad taking away an unexploded bomb from the doorway of the pub just down the road and collecting shrapnel in the street.

We were taken overnight to a rest centre in Kenilworth to sleep for about a week. There were no beds, just blankets on the floor. We were told then to go to Tile Hill station to be taken to a new place. We were taken to a little village called Hurley just outside of Kingsbury, and lived over a newsagent's shop for a week. Then, we were sent to a set of small farm cottages attached to a farm just down the road, where we lived for about six months. School was rather sporadic for me there as it was a 3-mile walk to Kingsbury, the closest one-room school, so I missed quite a lot. My father was called up from there, and after about six weeks he came home on leave. Little did we know it was embarkation leave, and we did not see him for over four years.

From the farm, we moved to Birmingham and out of immediate danger, living with a woman whose husband was also in the Army. We returned to Coventry in 1945 to live with my aunt. One night my mother, sister and I were all sleeping in the same room when my mum heard footsteps coming down the road. She sat up in bed and said, 'That's your dad'. Sure enough, she was right. My sister hid under the covers – she did not know him. He had been flown home from Italy and had no way of getting in touch with us. A happy reunion.

'Operation Sea Lion'

The so-called 'Operation Sea Lion' was the codename for Hitler's planned invasion of the British Isles in 1940.

Today, the plans for this attack are available to the public and present a frightening picture of what might have been. For several years, German intelligence had been gathering highly detailed information on Britain, meaning that the Nazis found it relatively easy to plan a course of action. Britain was analysed in terms of its physical geography: size, weather, roads and so on. Every aspect was considered in minute critical detail, from the undesirable location of factory workers' housing to the materials used in road surfacing. Photographs were taken of important sites, such as Windsor Castle and main city bridges, to add yet further detail and context. Britain was divided into areas, which were then assessed individually in terms of how easily troops might move around them. Some, such as the Midlands and Western Yorkshire, posed few difficulties, while others, such as 'The London Basin' and Wales, were far more problematic. To Hitler, the raid was seen as inevitable, and in Germany officials were being trained to take over administrative roles in Britain when the time came.

Civilians were made aware of the danger of invasion. The Ministry of Information, working with the War Office and Ministry of Home Security, issued civilians with instructions on what to do if the country was invaded. Instructions were practical and reassuring but did not shy away from presenting the dangers posed by enemy forces. The example of countries such as Holland and Belgium, where fleeing civilians were machine-gunned from the air, meant that British citizens were left in no doubt as to what suffering may lay ahead. People were asked to stay put in the event of an invasion, unless told otherwise, and to hide food, fuel and vehicles so that the enemy would be unable to take and use them.

Above all, they were asked to 'Think always of your country before you think of yourself.' The orders from Winston Churchill were to 'stand firm' and 'carry on'. The slogan and image 'Keep Calm and Carry On' has, in recent years, become an iconic signifier of the Second World War. In fact, the posters bearing this motto were never used. Many were printed and kept in storage, ready to be displayed as advice and reassurance as soon as the Nazis invaded Britain; so likely did an invasion seem. When this invasion did not come, they were discarded. What we now perceive as the ultimate archetypal wartime message was actually only seen by a small amount of people at the time.

Month Two

Day 31

A very busy day in the garden. As we enter March, there is far more
to be done in terms of planning and planting for the year's produce.
Today I have set first early seed potatoes to chit, planted out onions,
and sown cabbage and kale in seed trays indoors. Carried away by
finding some netting in an old trunk of miscellaneous garden items
(broken pots, pieces of plastic, wire …), I decided to net my raspberry
canes as protection against the birds. This is a bit premature, I know
– the canes don't need covering with net until there is actually some
fruit to protect, but this year I am taking no chances. Last year, the
birds ate all my raspberries and blackcurrants; a theft I took dearly
to heart.

Once I had the netting out on the ground, however, I realised that I
had absolutely no idea how I was meant to use it. None of my books
were forthcoming on the matter, so I resorted to guesswork, draping
the net over three hastily found sticks and burying the edges of it in
the ground. My main worry is that a bird may somehow find a way
in and become trapped underneath the netting, although I think it is
fairly safely secured.

It being a nice day, I took a break at lunchtime to do some more
of my washing. This is no less tedious than before, but I am finding
that keeping on top of it with a 'little and often' approach makes the
whole thing bearable.

After another lengthy stint in the garden, carrying on with more
tidying and clearing, I didn't feel at all like standing in front of the
cooker and making lamb and leek hotpot. The finished product is
delicious, but the prospect of a cup of tea and Thomas Hardy was
far more inviting. Nonetheless, the hotpot was made and much
appreciated. I'm not sure I've worked this hard in a very long time;
if nothing else, hopefully I will have become fitter by the end of the
year.

Day 32

According to a local newspaper report, almost half of the households
in Cornwall no longer eat together. Television and 'hectic lifestyles'
are to blame apparently, though I think television could probably

take the lion's share of this blame pie. Perhaps living in the war is making me more old-fashioned, but to me this seems an awful shame. Practices that have been continued for centuries are swiftly being lost in modern society, and while it might not seem an especially important thing to uphold, this seems to be yet another nail in the coffin of the traditional family unit. A report published only days earlier states that eating a family meal together for at least three days out of seven is the key to building strong bonds between parents and children.

I wonder if lax eating routines are contributing to the amount of convenience food that is consumed; or maybe this abundance of ready-made food is itself hastening the death of proper mealtimes. If a dish takes only three minutes in a microwave, there is far less need to wait and sit down with the rest of your household to enjoy it. In previous generations, there would be guilt associated with not taking time to appreciate food that someone has lovingly prepared.

It may sound judgemental, but I look at the food that other people buy in shops and wonder if society has really progressed as much as we think it has. There's no denying that junk food exists because there is a great demand for it, and that the demand is partly because people nowadays do not have either the time or motivation to cook from scratch every day. I've done it myself – coming home after a long day at work, the temptation to put a pizza in the microwave is sometimes overwhelming. I'm not suggesting that this shouldn't be an option every now and then; just that a nation of families living only on this kind of food is wrong. We live in a land of relative abundance, yet people are becoming ill from malnourishment when the nutrients they badly need are in the same shop as their high-fat, high-salt ready meals. It could never be done, and it would surely be wrong, but a small part of me wishes that the wide choice of food could be taken away from us as a society, and real ingredients put back on the menu. If there were no junk food, people would have to learn how to work with fresh ingredients on a daily basis.

Here endeth the lesson …

Day 34

Food rationing has now been introduced to my diet – on bacon, butter and sugar – but so far hasn't really affected me. Butter being rationed is something that has made me change my cooking slightly, but doesn't seem a crisis as I still have the option of lard, margarine and beef dripping. This seems a nice, gentle way to ease into rationing; I think the meat ration (coming into force within the next week or two) will be the first restriction to 'hurt'. Having changed my diet from a twenty-first-century one to that of a 1930s woman, I have naturally tended towards meat for evening meals, as many people did in those times. To become dependent on it as a failsafe meal option and then have it taken away is a little scary. I'm going to have to become far more inventive!

In the meantime, however, I still have the option of beef and champ (mashed potato with cabbage) for dinner. I'm a little shocked by the number of potatoes I seem to be getting through now; they were abundant during the war (well, compared to most other things), so generally featured in at least one meal a day, if not more. A Kitchen Front advertisement from 1940 declares, 'Think of the potato! Think of it as a weapon of war.' Potatoes were, essentially, one of the main foods that kept the country going.

Day 35

I have just sat down with several wartime cookbooks and planned out a menu for the week, making the most of the ingredients I have and allowing for no waste. I have to say, I'm feeling quite pleased with myself. One component every cookbook seems to be fascinated by is the 'winter salad', or 'vegetable salad'. The variation I'm opting for consists of cooked beetroot, potato, carrot and watercress or lettuce, with nut oil and vinegar dressing. The virtues of salads, and raw vegetables in general, seem to be extolled at every available opportunity, so it's about time I made a proper effort to try them.

Other dishes this week will include fish pie, braised steak with dumplings, and fish with leek sauce and parsley potato cakes. The leeks are to come from Ben's allotment, so feel especially wartime. I'm hoping that such forward planning will also encourage me to buy less, and so waste less food and spend less money. Going in with no real plan and a scattergun approach to groceries seems to result in a strange collection of items that frequently don't get used. Traditionally, before putting away the shopping on a Wednesday I would go through the fridge and throw away everything that had gone off or remained uneaten during the week before.

Day 38

Today was the first day of my planned week's menu. Dinner this evening was salmon with a white sauce and potato cakes. The potato cakes seemed to be going better than planned during the preparation stage, binding together well and retaining their shape. However, the breadcrumb coating had some reluctance when it came to sticking to the potato, meaning that there was an extremely thin and patchy covering that didn't crisp up as I'd imagined. The meal was very pleasant and different to what I normally eat, although I sense that the potato cakes are going to need a little more practice (and a little more seasoning, while we're at it).

I've been reading about the difficulty that convoys had in crossing the Atlantic to bring food to Britain. The number that were attacked and destroyed on the way is staggering, and really brings home the reason why food waste was so despised. If sailors died trying to bring food to those on the home front, it would have been galling to imagine that food being thrown into the rubbish bin. Nowadays, there isn't the same guilt of death tolls to deter the nation from wasting food, though I think that the 'waste not' habit is still a valuable one to get into.

Last year, I acquired a wormery for my garden through a local scheme to encourage residents to rethink how they deal with food waste. Wormeries are useful in that they can dispose of far more leftover products than a regular composter. Composters cannot take cooked food, whereas wormeries can. Similarly, worms do not object to meat scraps or breadcrumbs. During the war, homes saved any food scraps that they couldn't 'invent' dishes with to be used as pig food, meaning that everything had a use. It seems that wormeries could now be the modern equivalent, with the added bonus that their owners also get something back: high-quality compost and liquid fertiliser for their garden. Use that fertiliser to help along your vegetable patch and there's a charming 'circle of life' feel to the whole affair.

Day 40

Just a quick note to register my surprise at how delicious tonight's winter salad was. I was more than dubious about how tasty diced and boiled potato would be, but with the recommended nut and vinegar dressing, and combined with the carrot, beetroot and watercress, it was very tasty. I had cleared my plate of salad before finishing the pork, which must be a first. Who knew wartime cuisine could be this good?

Day 45
Today was the first day of meat rationing; gone are the days of thick steaks and roast chickens. Woe! For dinner this evening I made fishcakes, an interesting process if not necessarily a tasty one. Despite leaving them in a cool place for an hour after moulding into shape, the result was still extremely fragile and a bit too soft generally – like eating a lump of smooth paste rather than a fishcake as I'm used to them. Nonetheless, I do know that I'm lucky to have fish at all – it was never rationed but was often very hard to get as numbers of fishermen declined and coastlines became more dangerous. One family story I've been told is of my great-aunt being promised fish and chips for dinner one evening, while pregnant. Her husband, arriving at the chip shop, found that there had been no fish delivery and had to break the news to his wife that her 'fish supper' was minus fish. Presumably overwrought, hungry and hormonal, she burst into tears. It's amazing the effect that food has on morale.

This week's menu is obviously a lot leaner in terms of meat (pun intended I'm afraid). Cheese isn't yet on the ration, so one meat-free meal will be cheese and onion pie, which I've eaten before but never made myself. I can only hope that it'll be as nice as my memories of it. Bacon can also be factored into meal plans; the rationed amount is currently working out at around three standard rashers a week, which seems perfectly reasonable. It's harder to work out the meat ration as instead of being allocated by weight, it was measured in money at 1s 10d worth of meat per person, per week. Having spent a lot of time trying to work out the modern day equivalent to this, I ended up no nearer to an answer than before I started. Other sources, however, have estimated that a rough weight translation is around 500g per person. This obviously excludes 'luxury' meats such as steak, which weren't really available, or else would have been far more expensive – forcing buyers to choose between one small piece of very nice meat or a greater quantity of poorer meat. This week, my meat ration extended to some minced beef and a small amount of stewing lamb, which will be used for shepherd's pie and lamb hotpot respectively.

Other meals on the menu include macaroni with bacon, quiche and wholemeal scones. I'm really rather enjoying having to be more creative with what I make. Though this evening's meal wasn't particularly tasty, it's nice to try new ideas and test the boundaries of what I can do. It's so easy to get complacent when there's an endless supply of food from all seasons.

Day 48

Today, some friends and I went along to a local garden event that was held along a 'Dig for Victory' theme. A National Trust-owned garden nearby has adopted some allotment space and is growing crops typical of the wartime period. Next to the allotment is a replica Anderson shelter, built to the standard size for a small family. On a tour of this site, it became clear that many people today are keen on finding out more about growing their own vegetables – the day seemed to be very well attended, with lots of amateurs in addition to allotment enthusiasts. As our guide pointed out, the fact that there is no war on at present doesn't mean it isn't a wise idea to become more self-sufficient.

I was shocked to hear that when the Second World War broke out, if food supplies had been cut off immediately and entirely Britain had only enough resources to keep going for a matter of days. This really brought home why Dig for Victory was such an important campaign. Even aside from the interesting tour of the allotment, I very much enjoyed my day out. Sitting with friends and a picnic in a terrace garden was a lovely 'holidaying at home' way to spend a sunny afternoon. It could have been 2011 or 1811; the year didn't matter.

Day 50

It is very unfortunate that my renewed enthusiasm for Dig for Victory seems to have coincided with the possible death of my cabbage seedlings. Fearing that they were becoming too overcrowded in their seed tray, I potted them on. Now, however, they are extremely unhappy with me and in some cases are shrivelling up or turning yellow around the leaves. The prospect of them all dying is surprisingly disturbing to me – I'm relying on the crop for food in early summer and know that it may now be too late to start again. I'm keeping fingers crossed that this is just shock and not the death knell.

Day 56

I'm starting a new part-time job tomorrow so have had to think about ration-friendly packed lunches and faster evening meals that can be made when I get home. Working until now from home, I have had the option of taking a break mid-afternoon to begin cooking dinner, as many dishes take far longer than we're used to nowadays. In preparation for the lunches, I have made a tray of flapjacks to a wartime recipe that I was hoping should be filling and easy to take with me. The 'easy to take with me' part of this hope may not be fulfilled – as the recipe was based around using a minimum of ingredients, the amount of butter in it was far lower than usual flapjack recipes. As such, the mixture, though delicious raw, hasn't really bound together properly while cooking, leaving me with a tray of oaty crumbs. I'm going to have to eat them as best I can, as I don't have the fat left to make more and can't waste the ingredients. A bag of crumbs is much less dignified for public consumption than a flapjack wrapped in paper.

A baking failure in 1940 is far more upsetting than a baking failure in the twenty-first century; I think because the ingredients feel so scarce and precious, it seems such a shame to have gambled them on something that doesn't work. With the same amount of margarine and far less oats, I could have made the topping for a crumble that would have lasted me a few days as a dessert.

It'll be strange having to let the past and present worlds meet once again at work; I've got used to living in my own strange time-warp. I'm a bit worried that my new colleagues might think I'm odd – how on earth do I explain the thought processes behind living in the 1940s? At least the job is in the heritage sector, so I may find one or two people that are sympathetic to the cause.

Day 57

I must confess, after thinking that I was settling in very well to my new lifestyle, I'm starting to struggle. After a slightly stressful few days, I am longing to lounge in front of the television and eat crisps. I feel bored and a bit restless. During the course of my war so far, I have found a few activities that I enjoy, which form the 'relaxation' part of my day: listening to the radio, reading and knitting. Even these are failing to amuse me at the moment, which I suppose might be natural after two months of doing them almost daily.

Despite this wobble, I still managed to exercise some fairly decent self-control at a work training session today. Though the company brought along packaged sandwiches, crisps and cake, I ate my homemade cheese and salad sandwich and indulged only in two biscuits during the tea break. The chocolate cake and packets of crisps on offer were extremely tempting, and I even went as far as to take some crisps to my table before exerting discipline and putting them back.

A Week's Menu for February 1940

This week's menu has been designed to make the most of the ingredients I buy, aiming for no waste. At this time, the only food items rationed are butter, sugar and bacon. Meat is still un-rationed.

Day 1
Lunch: Egg and watercress sandwich
Dinner: Fish fillet with leeks in a white sauce, parsley potato cakes and salad

Day 2
Lunch: Scrambled eggs on toast
Dinner: Braised steak with dumplings, carrots and baked potato

Day 3
Lunch: Chicken and salad sandwich
Dinner: Pork chop with winter salad of carrot, potato, watercress and beetroot

Day 4
Lunch: Cheese sandwich
Dinner: Sea Pie (beef and vegetables with suet crust) with broccoli

---

Day 5
Lunch: Baked potato with salad
Dinner: Fish pie

Day 6
Lunch: Cheese and lettuce sandwich
Dinner: Bacon and cheese omelette with winter salad

Day 7
Lunch: Bacon sandwich
Dinner: Meat and potato pie

A Week's Menu for December 1940

By December 1940, many more items have become rationed, including meat. Cooks at home were forced to become far more creative with vegetables and meat-free options.

Day 1
Lunch: Wholemeal scone with salad
Dinner: Baked fish with boiled potatoes and salad

Day 2
Lunch: Egg sandwich
Dinner: Scalloped potatoes with bacon, served with cabbage

Day 3
Lunch: Leek and potato soup with a wholemeal scone
Dinner: Cheese and onion pie

Day 4
Lunch: Cheese and onion pie
Dinner: Cottage pie with carrots and cabbage

Day 5
Lunch: Baked potato with salad
Dinner: Macaroni with bacon and leek

Day 6
Lunch: Omelette with salad
Dinner: 'Champ' (potato and cabbage) with carrots

Day 7
Lunch: Poached eggs on toast
Dinner: Small pork chop with mashed potato and cabbage

Recipe Card: Winter Vegetable Salad

During the war, salad and raw vegetables were championed, with a salad suggested as the accompaniment to most meals. This recipe is my own spin on the salad theme, with the addition of cooked vegetables for cold winter days. If any of the ingredients are not available locally, simply leave them out. A winter salad should be an easy dish to tweak depending on whether it is early, mid- or late winter and on personal preference. Cress can be grown all year on a sunny windowsill with an absolute minimum of effort.

This makes a fresh and interesting accompaniment to many different dishes, such as meat, fish or quiche. Alternatively, make it a light meal or lunch by adding some chopped cooked chicken or sliced boiled eggs to the salad.

Ingredients:
Diced potato
Diced carrot
One or all of the following (depending on seasonality and
    availability): watercress, rocket, spinach, lettuce
Diced cooked beetroot
Celery

Cress
Vinegar
Olive oil or nut oil (I use walnut)
Salt
Pepper
Mustard (optional)
Sugar (optional)

Method:

Steam or boil the potato and carrot so that they are cooked, but not overcooked (overcooking is a major wartime no-no and 'washes out' the nutrients). If you prefer, the carrot can be served raw instead; simply grate or thinly slice it.

If you are using your own home-grown beetroot, cook this also; whole beetroot may take around thirty minutes to cook, but are ready when a knife can be inserted easily and when the skin rubs off. In most cases nowadays, the beetroot will be bought vacuum-packed and will be pre-cooked, so needs only to be sliced.

Drain the cooked vegetables and mix together with the raw leaves, cress and celery.

To make the dressing, pour out a small quantity of oil and mix with vinegar until it is to your own taste. Add a pinch of salt and pepper, and – if you like – mix in a small amount of mustard for an added kick. If the overall flavour is too harsh, add sugar to balance it out.

In the Kitchen Garden

One Sunday in mid-March I planted the parsnip seeds in a freshly dug and stone-free bed (parsnips prefer no stones) and prayed that the cats would leave them alone. Since I've dug this particular bed over, our cats seem to love digging in it. I've already found one onion bulb mysteriously lying on the top of the bed again. I think I may have to seek out a natural deterrent for this area, lest my winter crops be ruined before they've had a chance to begin. One suggestion that has been made is to thinly lie cut brambles over the surface of the bed, as the cats may not like to be among the prickles.

Leeks and autumn cabbage seeds were sown into a seed tray and placed on a windowsill indoors to 'get going', while lettuce and rocket leaves were sown straight into pots outdoors.

Space became the real issue, as an overly enthusiastic range of crops left me in doubt as to whether they'd all fit into the one remotely sunny part of the garden. Any leftover seedlings could go onto the allotment, but this lacks the convenience of harvesting from only metres away from the kitchen. After some careful and optimistic planning, everything seems to be accounted for in terms of space; everything, that is, apart from the potatoes. These categorically will not fit into the vegetable beds, and have had to seek alternative accommodation in old tyres, which can be stacked up as the soil level rises. A handful of leftover seed potatoes were 'guerilla planted' in odd spaces between shrubs and flowers, making the most of any available gap. The main thing now is to remember where these are buried!

One very welcome addition to the garden was a makeshift cold frame, which Ben constructed out of discarded blocks, old wood and a pane of greenhouse glass. My desperate need for extra 'indoor' space came upon me one day when searching for available room on a windowsill and finding none. It might not win any prizes for beauty, but I am delighted with my new-old cold frame, which has become invaluable and didn't cost a penny.

Things to do:
March
March is one of the busiest months in a kitchen gardener's calendar as there is so much to get going. Sow kale, oregano, radishes, purple sprouting broccoli, tomatoes, rocket, early autumn cabbages, onions, French beans, turnips, parsnips and leeks. Parsnips, turnips, onions, rocket and radishes can be planted directly into the ground, whereas it may be safer to plant the remaining vegetables listed in seed trays or under cover. If you are in a colder area, such as Scotland, it may be better to wait a few weeks longer than advised to sow seeds.

April
This is another busy planting month, as the weather becomes warmer and the risk of frost passes. Sow seeds under cover or indoors in a

propagator for runner beans, courgettes and winter cabbage varieties. If you live in a relatively mild climate, plant pea seeds directly into the ground; if it is colder, it may be wise to start the plants off under cover. Beetroot can now be sown directly into the ground, as can carrots.

Month Three

Day 62

Today is Mother's Day, something that we always celebrate as a family and a day that is increasingly becoming big business for greetings-card and gift companies. Bucking the spending trend and returning to more traditional methods, I baked my mother a cake (sacrificing all of my butter ration and part of the margarine) and made her a card. It's easily been ten years since I made a card myself, and though the end result was decidedly childlike, I think the effort was appreciated. When I was young, I was always encouraged to make cards for friends and relatives rather than buy them, but I have got out of the habit in recent years.

Though it may come across as stingy, it pleased me that I managed to mark the day without spending a lot of money in the shops.

Another practice that has been completely lost (until now) is that of letter writing. Keeping in the spirit of my wartime experiment, my friend Becky has started sending me letters. Ordinarily, we keep in touch by text message or through social networking, which is far easier and more frequent, but also more trivial. Writing a letter to Becky, I can take the time to think about what is being said and put more news in that may actually be interesting. What surprised me, however, was that partway through writing my letter my hand began to ache; reminding me what a shockingly long time is has been since I hand-wrote anything of considerable length.

Day 66

I'm beginning to feel a bit overbusy, trying to juggle my new job with my various existing writing commitments, in addition to the volunteer work that I've taken on for the charity shop and local history group. Having so much to do, I feel as if I am doing several things poorly and none of them (except my new job, as it has designated hours) especially well. A large chunk of what was previously my 'free time' is spent trying to keep each responsibility relatively well looked-after, but I know I'm not achieving this.

This book is also proving difficult at present: my lifestyle, particularly in terms of food, has become rather monotonous and I am struggling to find remotely interesting things to say about it. At this point, I'm seriously becoming worried that I won't get it done at all. But I'd hate to give up now, and would feel so disappointed with myself.

I know that during the war people had far more responsibilities to take care of. After a day at work – and hard work too – a woman of my age would be expected to cook dinner (perhaps interrupted by air raids) and then go back out to do voluntary work such as fire-watching, providing refreshments for bombed-out families or collecting donations of clothes. By griping in this way I feel as if I'm somehow insulting the memory of those women, who took on the copious amounts of work but also had the added risks of bombing, fire and blackout to contend with. Women serving in the Women's Voluntary Service (WVS) lost their lives or were badly injured while on duty.

Day 68
One thing to have come out of the war is that I am not sure I shall ever buy frozen oven chips again. One of my occasional treats is to make oven chips from scratch, cooked in beef dripping. They're surprisingly easy to do and take only around five or ten minutes longer than regular frozen oven chips.

Peel a potato (or if you're feeling particularly patriotic, don't) and slice it into chip-sized lengths. Boil the chips for around five minutes and while they are cooking put some solid beef dripping into an oven dish and put into the oven (on around 180°C) to melt and heat up. When this is done, put the chips into the fat, making sure that they are coated in it, and cook for around 25 minutes until they are cooked and golden brown.

While this is no good for vegetarians, the beef dripping makes very tasty chips and is the fat of choice for some fish and chip shops. I can't cook chips this way as often as I'd like due to the rationing of fats, but it certainly perks up a slow week. Compared to the price of a bag of oven chips, this method is far cheaper. In fact, it costs next to nothing for one large potato per person and a tub or pack of dripping that will last for months. While many people recommend using beef dripping in a deep fat fryer and making chips this way, as a 'wartime girl' I must advocate oven cooking as it uses far less fat.

Dripping seems to have fallen out of fashion in the modern day, but in my opinion it really deserves a comeback. Perhaps food gurus would argue that it is too unhealthy compared to the oils more commonly used now, but in moderation – particularly using wartime amounts – I don't see why it should be demonised. Another bonus is that it makes the most of an animal carcass and means that there is less waste. You can even 'make' your own dripping for free by collecting the fat that has run off a roasted beef or pork joint in the pan.

Day 69

With wine off the wartime menu, one of my favourite indulgences has been taken away. To make up for the loss, Ben and I are trying our hands at home brewing. The first project to be tried is home-made alcoholic ginger beer, made with dried ground ginger. The recipe we have found does not require too much sugar and should only take around three weeks of brewing before the final product is ready. At the moment, the 'plant' (the base of the beer) is fermenting in my bedroom, which is the warmest room in the house. In a week, this can then be added to sugared water and left to ferment in demijohns.

If this is a success (or even if it isn't), I have my eye on some country wine recipes that will make the most of free produce such as blackberries, elderflower, honeysuckle and rose petals. I have even found one for gorse wine, but can't bring myself to pick the lovely yellow flowers that are in the hedgerows hereabouts. They are so small that I imagine I'd have to deplete several bushes to get enough flowers, which look and smell beautiful.

Day 70

This evening I was invited out to a dinner party; a three-course meal of creamy mushroom soup, spaghetti bolognese and rich chocolate cake. Like a child in a sweet shop, I gorged on the modern-day food.

The bolognese in particular was something that I have been craving for a very long time, and so as not to let the opportunity pass me by I had two helpings. To wash it all down, I drank two glasses of red wine and felt very pleased with myself indeed.

A couple of hours later, I do not feel at all pleased with myself. I feel incredibly ill. It seems that, while I do not always like my wartime diet, my body has become very used to the plainer, more vegetable-dominated food and is extremely disgruntled at the sudden injection of fats. I will not be slipping off the ration again in such a hurry. This is the first real indication that things have changed in my life on a more long-term basis. I'm genuinely very surprised and have realised that when my self-imposed austerity period ends in just over nine months' time, I will have to remain careful about how quickly I reintroduce modern foods. In terms of learning, this has been a very useful evening – however, at this point in time I couldn't care less about the educational value of it and am content to lie curled up on my bed in self-pity.

Day 73

In the spirit of 'make do and mend' I have come up with a way of revitalising some very old and tired curtains. I'm not keen on the idea of throwing away my curtains, for two main reasons: they have plenty of life left in them and they have already been measured and cut to fit my awkward-sized windows. Nonetheless, something has to be done with them as they are badly faded in uneven patches.

As this fading is their main fault, I have bought some red dye which should give them a much-extended life span.

Day 80

My potatoes are growing at an absolutely alarming rate; almost faster than I can bank them up with earth. The unseasonably sunny weather that we have been having, followed by a rain shower, has seen them visibly shooting up in a matter of hours. The method of growing them in tyres has worked very well, as I can simply add a new tyre on top of the plants and fill it with earth. I am starting, however, to wonder just how many tyres the potatoes are going to require. They're currently at three tyres high and show no sign whatsoever of slowing down. I do hope this impressive display translates into a mammoth crop. I can't deny feeling a considerable amount of smugness at their progress, compared with those of some other people I know.

It's a pity the same can't be said for my tomato plants; slugs have got inside my cold frame overnight and totally decimated the seedlings. It's now back to the beginning for the tomato crop; I just hope it's not too late. It always surprises me how long the seeds take to grow.

Day 89

The last few days have been really tough; I'm not sure why, but all of a sudden the wartime way of life seems oppressive and unbearable. As my third month draws to a close, I feel totally lost and alienated from the culture that I have grown up in and lived in during my life so far. I know that this will sound ridiculously melodramatic, as millions of people live without all of the things that I have given up and barely think about it. It's very hard to explain how I feel – it's an annoying and slightly patronising phrase, but I think unless you have experienced this life it's probably hard to understand how big a culture shock it is. On paper, it sounds lovely and rather fun. In reality, my rose-tinted spectacles are now well and truly off. I am bored, sick of winter vegetables and fed up with cutting back on everything. I long to luxuriate in a deep, hot bath. There are so many good and fun things that have come out of this experience, but at this moment in time I am failing to appreciate them at all.

In a fit of bleakness and desperation, I have made the controversial decision to take a four-day break from the 1940s. Nobody can judge me more about this than I judge myself. It feels utterly wrong in so many ways; not least because the people living through a real war were in a far worse position than me, for a longer period of time, and had no option but to grit their teeth and carry on. In my gloom, I feel a failure. The driving force for the break is that I have stopped caring about what I'm doing and am not trying as hard as I should be. In the last couple of weeks, I have stopped making a proper effort at things; I've been 'guessing' my rationed weights on foods instead of weighing them out properly, and generally cutting corners wherever I can. Remembering how seriously I took these things at the start of the experiment, I see this as a very bad sign. I don't want to carry on knowing that I'm not doing my best, so the hope is that a break will allow me to rest, recharge my enthusiasm and start again – properly. No more corner cutting.

Recipe Card: Wartime Pudding

This recipe was created by a woman named Laurinda Donald during the war, and found in a scrapbook passed by her to my grandmother, and by my grandmother to my mother. Written in pencil next to it are the words 'own recipe, very good'.

Ingredients:
12 oz/340 g self-raising flour
4 oz/115 g suet
1 egg
Half tsp cinnamon
3 oz/85 g sugar
A few sultanas, or whatever can be spared
Pinch nutmeg
Pinch salt

Method:
Mix the flour, suet, salt, fruit, nutmeg, cinnamon and sugar and stir together. Beat in the egg and mix well.

Grease a pudding basin (these seem to be experiencing a surge in popularity nowadays) and pour in the mixture. Cover with a circle of greaseproof paper and wrap the basin (or at least, the top of it) with tin foil. The pudding should then be steamed for around two hours.

If you have a steamer, simply fill the bottom with water, place the pudding inside and steam as you normally would. If not, the steaming can be done in an oven. Place the pudding basin in a deep baking tray and fill the tray with water until it reaches halfway up the basin and cover the whole tray (including the basin) with foil. Alternatively, a pan of boiling water can be used – place something in the bottom of the pan, such as a wire rack or roll of tin foil, so that the pudding will not have contact with the hob and fill the pan with water until it comes halfway up the basin. Boil for two hours, regularly checking the water level.

When the time has elapsed, remove carefully with oven gloves. Some people prefer to attach a string 'handle' around the pudding before cooking to make this part of the process easier, though making the handle itself can also be fiddly.

Top Tips for Reducing Waste

1 Plan a weekly menu for meals before you go grocery shopping. This prevents you from buying unnecessary items and allows you to see where leftover food can be used up over other days.

2 Fix up and mend items that you might otherwise throw away or replace. This may require a bit of creativity and some very basic DIY skills, but can be very rewarding. It's also amazing what a simple lick of paint or varnish can do for many things.

3 Be careful to switch off lights when you are not in a room. Not only does this save energy, it also saves money on fuel bills. During the war, families were encouraged to use as little fuel as possible and given fuel-usage targets to meet.

4 Cook from scratch as much as possible. Avoiding ready-made or 'cheat's' food items almost always saves money and packaging, as well as being healthier. Often, dishes can be created from scratch using ingredients already in the house from other meals.

5 Place a dish in your sink for when you are washing things such as vegetables or your hands (not with handwash). The water collected in it might not be suitable for drinking or cooking, but it can be transferred to a watering can and used in the garden. If you can, install a water butt outside to collect rain water.

6 Invest in a composter or wormery. This will instantly make a healthy dent in the amount of waste that goes into your bin each week. Composting can give a new purpose to many waste items, such as paper, vegetable peelings, tea leaves, dead flowers and grass cuttings.

7 Find a new purpose for 'waste' items. I have grown potatoes in old tyres and used plastic containers as seed trays, with lemonade-bottle cloches as lids.

8 Save money and reuse paper by making your own greetings cards with wrapping paper, magazine or newspaper scraps. The end result might not be a perfect work of art, but family and friends will appreciate the effort you have made.

9 Buying food items that are seasonal and local reduces 'food miles' and saves the fuel that would be used to transport them. This

might not be a saving that seems to directly affect you, but it is an important one nonetheless.

10 Try using household products as cleaners to save money on expensive chemicals. Old favourites such as vinegar and newspaper for cleaning windows were once favourites for a reason. Bicarbonate of soda is an excellent all-rounder and can be used for scrubbing, eliminating bad smells and removing stains.

Items Rationed by December 1940

Bacon and ham: 4 oz per week
Sugar: 8 oz per week
Cooking fats (butter, lard, margarine, etc.): 8 oz in total per week
Meat: to the value of 1s 10d per week
Tea: 2 oz per week

CHAPTER THREE: 1941

The Spam Era (May–June)

In 1941

6 January: The meat ration is reduced – instead of purchasing meat to the value of 1s 10d, each person may now purchase meat to the value of 1s 6d each week

13 January: The meat ration is once again reduced, to the value of 1s 2d per week

27 January: The US ambassador to Japan reports hearing a rumour that a surprise attack on Pearl Harbor has been planned.

February: During this month, national wheatmeal bread – bread made from a higher percentage of whole grain and sold at a fixed price – is gradually introduced. This would later become known as the much-maligned National Loaf.

10 February: Unemployment reaches a record low, with 923,251 fewer people unemployed than this time last year.

19 February: Beginning of the 'Swansea Blitz': three consecutive nights of fierce bombing over Swansea.

11 March: The Lease and Lend Bill is passed in the United States, allowing America to export war materials and supplies to the UK, Soviet Union, France, China and other Allied countries. As well as aircraft and weapons, Britain is also able to receive food supplies such as tinned goods. This marks the end of America's supposed neutrality and the beginning of aggression from Germany towards the US.

17 March: Jam, treacle, syrup and marmalade are rationed as a group of foods: the 'sweet bread spreads'. Each person is allowed an overall 8 oz per month (2 oz per week) from this group. People are, however, able to buy two months' ration in advance as the usual weight of a jar or tin is 1 lb.

31 March: Meat ration reduced to meat to the value of 1s per week.

15 April: Belfast is subjected to a heavy bombing raid, with great damage being caused.

16 April: In the worst raid on London since the beginning of the Blitz, six German bombers are brought down over the city. Large fires are caused by incendiary bombs, and eight hospitals and many churches are destroyed in the night-long attack.

5 May: Cheese is added to the list of rationed goods at 1 oz per person, per week.

10–11 May: London suffers a heavy overnight air raid, the last major bombing in the capital of the first Blitz. Among the historic buildings damaged are the Houses of Parliament, Westminster Abbey and the British Museum. The clock face of Big Ben is blackened and damaged, but the great clock's hands continue to keep time. On the same evening, Hitler's deputy Führer Rudolf Hess flies from Germany to Scotland, crashing near Glasgow, in an apparent attempt to discuss peace. Hess is 'rounded up' by a ploughman and handed over to the Home Guard. Hitler, said to be furious, circulates reports that Hess is suffering from 'mental disorder'.

27 May: The German battleship *Bismarck* comes under heavy attack and sinks in the North Atlantic, killing almost 2,000 of its crew.

31 May: The first shipment of food from America, including over 4 million eggs, 120,000 lb of cheese and 1,000 tons of flour, arrives in the UK. Lord Woolton, the Minister of Food, officially receives the food on board the ship on behalf of the British Government.

1 June: The Board of Trade announces the immediate rationing of clothing and footwear. Each person is allocated sixty-six clothing coupons per year. It is now illegal to buy clothing, cloth, wool or footwear without handing over coupons. One exception is that clothing sized for children aged below four years can be purchased coupon-free.

30 June: Eggs are now rationed, at one per week (though this is not guaranteed) and the cheese ration increased to 2 oz per person, per week. A double ration of sugar is available to each person for four weeks, to allow for jam making at home. The butter ration is reduced from 4 oz to 2 oz, though the total fat ration remains at 8 oz. In addition to 2 oz butter, each person may purchase 6 oz of margarine, or 4 oz margarine and 2 oz cooking fat (e.g. lard). The price of fish, an un-rationed item, is fixed at a low price to prevent unfairly high charges. The price is roughly a third cheaper than the previous month.

7 July: Meat ration is increased to match the value of 1s 2d per week.

25 August: Cheese ration increased from 2 oz per week to 3 oz. Vegetarians and those employed in manual labour, such as agriculture, are entitled to a special large cheese ration of 8 oz per week.

6 September: In Germany and all German-occupied places, all Jews

over the age of six are now required to wear the Star of David as identification.

17 November: The fats ration is temporarily increased from 8 oz per week to 12 oz, and sugar temporarily increased from 8 oz per week to 10 oz.

23 November: Due to a shortage in milk, each adult is restricted to 2 pints per week – Lord Woolton adds that he cannot promise this amount; it is instead a target for dairymen to try and reach.

1 December: Tinned foods, such as meats, fish and beans, are once again available in the shops, under the new points rationing system. Goods such as these are given a points value, and each person allocated 16 points to 'spend' each month. Also available from today is national household milk powder, at one tin per family per month.

6 December: Britain declares war on Finland after the country demonstrates its allegiance to Germany.

7 December: The Japanese launch a surprise attack on Pearl Harbor, the base of the US Pacific Fleet. Four of America's battleships are sunk, along with 188 aircraft, three destroyers, three cruisers and an anti-aircraft training vessel. Over 2,400 people are killed and many more injured.

8 December: The United Kingdom and United States officially declare war on Japan.

15 December: The larger cheese ration for vegetarians and manual workers is increased from 8 oz per week to 12 oz per week.

29 December: The meat ration is changed to include tinned corned beef as compulsory. Each person remains entitled to meat to the value of 1s 2d per week, but one seventh (2d) must be taken as corned beef.

Meeting the Deficit

The year 1941 saw major changes to the nation's diet as food rationing came into full force. Former staples such as meat, eggs, cheese and milk became scarcer. Though meat had been rationed since 1940, the amount allowed per week fell steadily throughout the first three months of the year to become almost half of what it had been before. Cheese – an easy replacement for meat – became rationed in May 1941, with eggs following suit less than two months later.

In January, the Ministry of Food, foreseeing this problem, began promoting the increased consumption of foods that were in plentiful supply. The UK had experienced its largest crop of potatoes in years, leading to yet more carefully targeted discussion of the health benefits of this root vegetable. Carrots were also in abundance, and were praised for their skin-boosting properties and protection against winter illnesses. In newspaper advertisements, the Ministry of Food made suggestions of how people might use more carrots and potatoes. Ideas included carrot sandwiches, in which grated carrot was mixed with grated raw cabbage and chutney, and a carrot-cap salad featuring grated carrot, cooked diced potato and lettuce leaves.

One of the more unusual so-called benefits of the carrot was its ability to improve night vision. This is a fact now widely discredited, though at the time the RAF's success in shooting down enemy bombers was attributed to raw carrots, which supposedly helped them see in the dark. In fact, the humble carrot was covering the secret use of radar technology.

Other foods suggested to fill the gap included oatmeal (rich in Vitamin B1 and iron) and home-raised rabbits. In a radio broadcast, Lord Woolton appealed for householders to 'go easy with the tin opener' and instead make the most of supplies grown at home. People were asked to replace bread with potatoes, as importing flour occupied valuable shipping space. Instead of eating imported breakfast cereals, Lord Woolton asked that cooks returned to the old practice of making porridge with oats.

In addition to wrangling with shortages and restrictions, people also faced a general increase in expense. Though the prices of many scarce items were fixed to avoid overpricing by shops, the cost of living rose. Even potatoes, the most patriotic of vegetables, experienced an increase of ten shillings per ton in growers' prices in January 1941.

Studies were conducted to examine how an average low-income family might be faring in these times. It was estimated that a family of five (mother, father and three young children) would need around 69 shillings (£3 9s) a week to live: 30s 8d for food, 8s 6d for rent, 11s 1d for clothing (pre-rationing), 5s 4d for fuel and light and 13s 5d for sundries. For an average husband and wife of pension age, the weekly cost of living was around 38s 4d (almost £2). The wage of an average working man was between 70 and 75 shillings a week. Though the cost of living had risen since the beginning of war, the average wage had also increased due to the greater opportunity for work and overtime. In 1936, the average wage for a male was around 60 shillings; between 10 and 15 shillings lower than 1941.

While individuals continued to live somewhat within their means, the nation as a whole was on a major spending spree. By February 1941, the national expenditure had reached £12,250,000 a day, £10,500,000 of which was spent on fighting or war services. Estimated expenditure for the year was a staggering £4,000,000,000. Though the yearly national income was said to have risen around £2,000,000,000, there was nonetheless a large deficit, with more supplies of every kind desperately needed.

Despite the best efforts of all, it was becoming clear that the UK was struggling. In sharp contrast to this austerity was America, the land of plenty. Not yet a part of the war, the US had food – and ships, aeroplanes, tanks and guns – to spare.

On 9 January, 'all-out aid' to Britain, Greece and China was discussed in the White House, on President Roosevelt's recommendation. A 'Lease-and-Lend Bill' was put forward, beginning a programme of aid to those fighting the Axis. This pledge was promoted as an Act to promote the defence of the United States. Though primarily dealing with the defence and sustainability of other countries, this Act aimed to make the States a hub of democracy. The defence of other nations such as Britain was interpreted as integral to the defence of America. This aid was not necessarily free, however; the United States declared that there may be 'payment, or repayment in kind or property, or any other direct or indirect benefit which the President deems satisfactory'.

Initially, in its early form, the focus of America's aid was geared towards weapons, vehicles and other 'defence articles', rather than everyday supplies such as food. Admitting that Britain needed help was a controversial thing to do. Many pushing for urgent American aid to the UK were accused of predicting defeat by the Germans. This criticism fell heavily on Joseph Kennedy, the retiring American Ambassador to Britain, who advocated aid but was vocal in his desire to keep America out of the war.

In a speech defending himself, Kennedy said,

> The favourite device of [an] aggressive minority is to call any American questioning the likelihood of a British victory an apostle of gloom – a defeatist ... I know many of Britain's weaknesses, but a prediction can be based only on complete knowledge of the strengths and weaknesses of both sides. The morale of the British nation defies description. It is as fine a display of human courage as was ever witnessed. But what do we know about the morale of the German Army or of the German people? Thus the prediction now of England's defeat would be a senseless one. One can recognise the enormous difficulties facing Britain without foreseeing her defeat.

In defending what some saw as a failing Britain, the United States was putting itself in a difficult situation. Wishing to stay out of the war, America had to take great care when deciding to what extent it would help. Certain things, such as using American vessels on convoy duty – escorting ships across the Atlantic to Britain – could be seen as an act of war against the Germans. Indeed, after the Lease and Lend Bill was passed, a spokesman for Germany launched a scathing verbal attack on Roosevelt and 'the United States' self-appointed role of world arbitrator'. Hitler declared that all vessels carrying goods to Britain would be sunk.

Though a defeatist attitude was frowned upon, it was announced in October 1941 that provisions were being made to secure food in the event of invasion. Lord Woolton explained to the nation that, should the invader come, he had appointed local men and women to become 'Ministers of Food' in their districts. These ministers would be responsible for conducting a swift stock-take of local shops before overseeing the distribution of food locally. It was advised, however, that each household should not hoard food, and should only provision enough for a maximum of two weeks.

Though increased quantities of defence articles were a priority, American food was nonetheless to become a vital import to the people living on the home front. In the three months of discussion around the Lease and Lend Bill, an amendment was made to the proposed terms to include a provision for sending food to Britain. America's food stores were, said President Roosevelt, large enough to feed both his country and that of its friends. Agricultural commodities were classified as defence articles and as such could be sent out to those countries in need.

During March, discussions took place in America to ascertain the types and quantities of food that might be sent to the UK. By the end of May 1941 this food had begun to arrive; among the first deliveries were eggs, cheese and flour. Also bought from America were pork products, lard, wheat, powdered milk, dried eggs, tinned and dried fruit, dried beans, tinned fish, soups, tobacco and cotton. Though America was the main exporter of food, it was not alone in supplementing British stocks. From Canada came apples and larger shipments of bacon, while Australia sent cargoes of dried fruit, butter, tea and flour.

With more tinned and dried food arriving each month, a system had to be put into place to manage its distribution. At the beginning of December, points rationing was introduced. This helped to maintain supplies and ensure that each person was able to have their share of them. A pink points ration book was introduced, with each person being allocated sixteen points per four weeks. The points rationing system did not guarantee availability of a specific food, for instance, tinned salmon, but did secure an entitlement to enough food to spend your sixteen points. Though these points didn't stretch far by modern standards, the system heralded a welcome addition to the nation's diet. With meat, cheese and eggs in short supply, a tin of luncheon meat or fish added much-needed variety to meals.

One of the most exciting new products to become available was Spam. Unveiling this new meat, along with others such as Mor (minced pork shoulder), the Ministry of Food held a tasting session to introduce it to the nation. New recipes were tested and demonstrated to help demonstrate their usefulness and versatility. Spam would go on to become one of the archetypal foods of the war; often maligned but remembered fondly by millions.

Typical Points Values in December 1941 (per Pound)

16: Canned or bottled tongue, brisket, Australian minced meat loaf, Australian or New Zealand rabbit, Eire stewed steak, United States luncheon meat, US pork sausage, salmon, lobster, crayfish and sardines.
12: All other canned fish, such as herrings and pilchards.
8: All canned British meat products.
4: Canned beans in sauce or gravy.

Clothing is Rationed

With the introduction of clothes rationing in June, the nation was forced to become as frugal in dress as in food. Each person was granted an allowance of sixty-six coupons per year, which were not just compulsory for buying clothes, but were also needed for cloth, wool and shoes. The introduction of coupons was forced by a shortage in materials for making clothes, as most, such as wool and cotton, had to be imported and factories and workers were needed to produce vital war supplies. The clothes rationing system was designed by the Board of Trade to ensure that each person was able to purchase, on average, one set of new clothes each year. As with food rationing, the restrictions helped to make sure that everyone, regardless of wealth or social status, was able to receive their fair share of what was available. No notice was given, and clothing ration books were not distributed in advance of the announcement that rationing had begun. The general public was not warned in order to avoid a rush on buying clothing.

To begin with, in the absence of clothing ration books, consumers were asked to use up twenty-six old margarine coupons from their food ration books when paying for clothing. Once these had run out, they could then exchange the book for a new clothing card with forty coupons on – making a full sixty-six coupons in total for the year ending 31 May 1942. The first forty-six coupons could be used at any time and in any quantity, but the final twenty were marked with an X and had to be reserved until after 1 January 1942. This was in order to spread the demand for clothes.

Because children grow rapidly and their clothing required less material, children's clothing generally had a lower coupon value than adults'. Uniform for Officers and Cadets of the Royal Navy, Army and Air Force (including females such as those in the WAAF) could be purchased without coupons. Those who were bombed out of their homes, losing their clothing, could apply for extra coupons if their supply was considered lower than the 'essential requirements'. In this situation, a bombed-out person would be asked to list which items of clothing, if any, they still had so that an assessor could judge if they were in need of more.

The rules surrounding clothes rationing were strict. Shops willing to sell without coupons could face heavy penalties, and even second-hand clothing had to be bought within the confines of rationing, as if new. Those hoping to pick up extra items at charity bazaars and jumble sales were disappointed; from 5 August, no clothes or shoes could be bought without the surrender of coupons. However, if second-hand items were sold at a price below a certain scale, they could become coupon-free. As with food rationing, the system was complicated and difficult for the majority of people to get to grips with.

There were many complaints about the rationing system during its early days. Flaws were exposed, particularly in terms of work and uniforms, that needed more careful attention – a nurse entering hospital service, for instance, would need a total of eighty coupons, twelve more than her year's allowance, for her uniform alone. Women who liked to knit garments for soldiers serving overseas were disappointed and frustrated that they would have to present coupons when buying their wool, as many knitted far more items than the system allowed, even if they spent their sixty-six coupons on wool alone. Knitting clothes instead of buying them still involved coupons – in the early days of clothes rationing, one coupon was needed for every 2 oz wool purchased. This complaint was swiftly quashed only days later with the assurance that those knitting for official organisations such as the Royal Naval War Comforts Committee would be permitted to receive wool coupon-free if the fruits of their labours were returned as payment. Nonetheless, retailers reported a dramatic drop in sales of wool in service colours.

Men seeking to buy themselves a new suit were forced to face the reality that if they did so they would have no coupons leftover for basic items such as socks and handkerchiefs. On this subject, the Board of Trade stood firm, declaring, 'We are sympathetic, but such people will have to help themselves out of the difficulty. The scheme was based on the assumption that people have some wardrobe, and the ration is a replacement ration, not a fitting-out ration.' In sum, if you weren't well-dressed before the war, you certainly wouldn't be during the rest of it.

Shabby garments became branded 'honourable' and the wearing of older clothes was promoted by Oliver Lyttelton, President of the Board of Trade. Mr Lyttelton said,

> I know all the women will look smart, but we men may look shabby. If we do, we must not be ashamed. In war the term 'battle-stained' is an honourable one. People admire the solider whose uniform bears the marks of battle, or the fireman who is begrimed with his night's work. We must learn, as civilians, that it is also honourable to be seen in clothes which are not so smart, because we are bearing, as civilians, yet another share in the war if we too are battle-stained. When you feel tired of your old clothes, remember that by making them do you are contributing some part of an aeroplane or a gun or a tank, or, perhaps even more simply, an overcoat to one of our fighting men.

With less opportunity for new clothes, preserving the ones you already had became far more important. The popular slogan 'make do and mend' came into force with clothes rationing. This campaign encouraged women to take better care of clothing in order to prolong its life, and to make new items from those that were beyond repair or no longer needed. Old material, such as unwanted curtains or bedding, could be used for new clothes. Knitted items were unravelled so that the wool could be reused. Ingenious brides even made their wedding dresses from discarded parachute silk. Where no materials were available, women improvised even more by essentially making something from nothing; instead of new stockings, many coloured their legs with substances such as gravy browning, adding a pretend seam with eyeliner.

'Utility clothing', introduced towards the end of 1941, changed the way the public looked, with a new focus on simplicity and functionality over stylishness. Maximum prices and profit margins were introduced to keep clothing affordable, while a new set of regulations governed how much material could be used to cut down on waste. One of the 'utility cloths' that were controlled in terms of quality and price was woollen tweed, which, when made into a man's suit, was not allowed to exceed 59s 11d in price.

The Board of Trade was keen to emphasise that utility clothing did not mean that there would be a lack of variety in outfits. Introducing the idea of a change in clothing style, the Board promoted the wide range of patterns and colours that would be available, as well as the controlling of prices. Also controlled, however, were the length of hemlines, size of pockets, decorations on underwear and even the height of men's socks. Turn-ups were banned on trousers to much consternation. Items of clothing had to be made to government patterns and were marked with a CC41 logo, which stood for Civilian Clothing (41 being the year this scheme was introduced). This scheme became far more widespread in 1942, when it became illegal to use unnecessary embellishments on clothing. Fashions for women became tailored and slimline, with straight skirts that ended below the knee and simple, close-fitting tops. Men wore two-piece suits instead of three-piece, as the waistcoat fell out of favour. Also banned were double-breasted coats and men's sleeve buttons.

Even those serving in the forces were not immune; the regulation pattern of officers' service dress was changed by the War Office, though not substantially. Breast pockets could no longer have box pleats, and pocket styles were altered to use slightly less material.

Typical Clothes Coupon Values for June 1941

Men:
Mackintosh or raincoat: 16
Coat, jacket or blazer: 13
Unlined mackintosh or cape: 9

Trousers (other than fustian or corduroy) or kilt: 8
Nightshirt or pair of pyjamas: 8
Dressing gown: 8
Pair of shoes or boots: 7
Overalls or dungarees: 6
Fustian or corduroy trousers: 5
Waistcoat, cardigan, jersey or pullover: 5
Shorts: 5
Pair of socks or bathing trunks: 3
Pair of leggings, gaiters or spats: 3
Scarf, pair of gloves or mittens: 2
Two handkerchiefs: 1
Collar, tie or pair of cuffs: 1

Women:
Raincoat or coat (over 28 inches in length): 14
Jacket, blazer or short coat: 11
Woollen dress or gown: 11
Dress or gown of other materials: 7
Unlined mackintosh or cape: 9
Dressing gown: 8
Slacks: 8
Skirt: 7
Furs: 5
Blouse, sports shirt, jumper or bed jacket: 5
Boots, shoes or slippers: 5
Petticoat, slip or cami-knickers: 4
Apron or pinafore: 3
Scarf, pair of gloves, mittens or muff: 2
Pair of socks or stockings: 2
Pair of socks (ankle length): 1

Cloth:
Wool (cloth containing more than 15 per cent wool) per yard:
3 inches–9 inches wide: ½
9 inches–15 inches wide: 1

15 inches–21 inches wide: 1½
Increasing by a half coupon for every six-inches (e.g. 2 coupons for anything between 21 inches and 27 inches, 2½ for 27 inches–33 inches)

Other cloth except jute per yard:
3 inches–9 inches wide: ⅓
9 inches–5 inches: ⅔
15 inches–21 inches: 1
Increasing by a third of a coupon for every six inches. When a fraction of a coupon was used, this was generally rounded up to the nearest whole coupon.

Month Four

Day 97
Today, while out walking along a cliff path, I noticed that Ben and I were passing a huge number of flowering gorse bushes. I remembered reading in an old book about home brewing that the flowers could be used to make wine – it stuck in my memory as one of the less disgusting-sounding concoctions. Luckily, I had a bag to hand and we began picking the flowers. This turned out to be an extremely slow and prickly task, as it takes an age to collect enough flowers for brewing. Not having the book to hand, I had to guess how many would be enough – in the end we compromised at a point where we had a relatively full bag and distressingly windswept hair.

Back at home, we tipped our yellow blooms (around 2.5 litres in volume) into a large pan and added just under a gallon of water – as much as would conservatively fit in the pan, which is the largest I own. The process, put into our hands, is not an especially precise art. The mixture was brought to the boil and simmered for around twenty minutes. Disappointingly, at this point the gorse lost its delicious coconut smell and simply reminded me of undergrowth. When the mixture had cooled a little (so it is no longer boiling), we added around 800 g of sugar and let it dissolve in – at this point, the liquid began inexplicably to smell like tinned peaches. It may be down to the fact that I do not have an especially sweet tooth, but I have found that the sugar ration per week is far more than I could ever use – meaning that over a few weeks I have easily saved up enough for the recipe. After further cooling (allow it to become lukewarm), brewing yeast was added and the alarmingly yellow 'wine' left to its own devices. It is now busy fermenting (and smelling like peaches) and will continue to do so for a few more days.

Day 100
Our gorse-flower wine (well, not quite wine yet) has been transferred to a demijohn to continue brewing. The quantities we used have half-filled the container, leaving us to wish we had held out a little longer with the flower picking to make more. If anyone was considering trying the process, it might be wise to double what we have done – I would imagine that a plastic carrier bag, almost filled, would probably be a rough idea of how many flowers are needed. Though picking the flowers can be tedious – and painful if you let your guard down – on a nice and sunny day, I can imagine that it may have the potential to be quite pleasant. The principle that we were careful to stick to was not to pick too many flowers from just one bush, but to spread the picking over many so as to leave the area essentially unchanged.

Perhaps the war is making me stingy (a thought that occurs to me quite often now), but there is something very rewarding about making things for free. The only items purchased to make our wine are sugar and yeast, which are fairly cheap compared to the price of a bottle of the finished product. I also feel that it is nice to carry on old country customs such as this, as they are in danger of dying out in the future. Of course, our gorse-flower wine may turn out to be disgusting, in which case I could end up taking back these words ...

Day 102
My first foray into foraging has left me wanting more, so I have been researching edible wild plants that could easily be found near to where I live. After my wobble with the wartime way of life last month, it is nice to find something that offers a more fun

dimension to what I eat. To begin with, I am focusing on things that are very easily and definitely identifiable, as I am not keen on picking things I'm uncertain of. The two easiest candidates for me are stinging nettles and three-cornered leek (*Allium triquetrum*). Stinging nettles are all-too-easy to find nearby, while three-cornered leek grows vigorously in my back garden. For years, I have tried to eradicate this invasive and smelly plant, though it does put out beautiful white bell-shaped flowers in the spring. A relation of the more commonly found wild garlic, three-cornered leek has a taste more akin to onions – or, not surprisingly, leeks. It seems only fair that, as a consolation prize for being stuck with the ever-spreading plant, I should be able to eat some of the leaves. I have learned that young leaves can be chopped up and used raw in salads, but those in my back garden have grown more mature and are now best suited to cooking as vegetables; much as you might use onions or leeks. Three-cornered leek can be identified by its stem, which is triangular, and by its distinctive onion smell (if you think you have found three-cornered leek it is probably best to make sure before eating it).

During the war, the Ministry of Food actively encouraged people to make the most of a 'hedgerow harvest', publishing leaflets containing advice and recipes to make foraging easy and worthwhile.

This afternoon, between rain showers, I walked down the lane to my grandmother's house, picking stinging nettle leaves as I went. I suspect I made a strange sight – leaning into brambly hedges and walking along with one gardening glove on. I went for the small, young leaves on each plant as apparently the more mature leaves are gritty and can be bad for you. My foraged goods have been washed and are ready to use in tomorrow's cooking. For tea today, I made a quiche lorraine (my entire bacon ration is now gone) and an apple crumble (likewise my butter ration).

Day 103

The next chapter of my home-brewing adventure has begun – this time it is honeysuckle wine. Stuck for something to do this afternoon, Ben and I fell upon the idea while looking at a very large and overgrown honeysuckle in the garden. I've been meaning to quite vigorously prune it for some time, but have been putting off the job until the flowers finish as they look so pretty. It was very easy to collect enough flowers, and far less painful than picking gorse. Even now, it is hard to see that any are missing from the honeysuckle's vast expanse. To make things easy, we have followed the same recipe and quantities as those for gorse wine. The only change has been that when adding the sugar to the mixture, we also added a cup of very strong black tea. The finished liquid can also be transferred to the demijohn much sooner than the gorse wine – instead of waiting three or four days it can be moved on after it has cooled.

Disappointingly, my new-found passion for making country wines will now have to be stopped in its tracks until I can save up enough sugar from the ration to begin again.

Today, I went to my favourite café for lunch as a treat, and I was delighted to find that my side salad included the flowers from a three-cornered leek. It seems that more and more people are moving over to the idea of thrifty and seasonal cooking. My lunch was delicious and very attractive, with its small white flowers as edible decoration.

Day 104

For dinner this evening, I cooked fish with a home-made stinging-nettle pesto. My basil plant is now getting large enough to use, so the two main ingredients were free and freshly picked. Pasta with pesto was one of my favourite pre-war dishes, and I have been sorely missing pesto ever since. My one reservation is that I'm not 100 per cent confident that in wartime people would have had basil seeds, as basil is not native to the UK and is unlikely (as a non-essential) to have been imported. However, I had seeds left over from last year and didn't want to waste them – besides, it seems a shame not to eat food that is healthy and home-grown, particularly as it fits so well with the Dig for Victory ethos. This is one modern-day twist on the experiment that I don't count as 'proper cheating' (if it even is cheating). My research suggests that before the war, many herbs not native to the UK were imported, and that during the war groups of people made themselves responsible for growing or gathering herbs to use medicinally.

Recipe Card: Stinging-Nettle Pesto

Makes enough to coat two small salmon fillets or mix with a generous portion of pasta (if you have some).

Ingredients:
A large (gloved) handful of young stinging-nettle leaves
1 tbsp chopped fresh basil
1 garlic clove
1–2 tsp grated cheese
Walnut or olive oil (I have used walnut oil)
Pinch salt

Method:
Thoroughly wash your stinging nettles in cold water and check for any bugs that might be lingering. Bring a pan of salted water to the boil and add the nettles – cook for 2–3 minutes. Drain the nettles and rinse with cold water in a colander. Press them with the back of a spoon to strain out any excess water. You could keep the cooking water as a compost accelerant or for nettle tea.

Chop the nettle leaves and garlic and mix with the chopped basil, salt and cheese. Grind in a pestle and mortar or use a food processor if you live in modern times. Add enough oil to make the pesto the consistency that you like it.

Use straight away or refrigerate until needed.

If it is the right time of year and you are keen to exploit a 'hedgerow harvest', the chopped garlic clove could be replaced by chopped wild garlic. Sea beet, or sea spinach, grows along the coast in some areas and is another spinach-like wild plant that could be used in this recipe instead of stinging nettles.

Day 110

Never ones to let a weekend pass by unworked, today Ben and I set about clearing a desperately overgrown area in the back garden. A patch around the pond has long been lost to grasses and brambles, and always seemed too large a job to contemplate. However, in a quest to free up more room for vegetables, we took on the task and found it to be every bit as tough as expected. A few hours (and several sacks of green waste) later, I have a large bed that can be turned over to production.

Part of me very much wanted to devote the area to summer bedding plants, but practicality has prevailed and I have already sown more pea seeds in it. As a compromise, I'm going to interplant the peas with sweet pea seeds, as they can climb up the same canes. Sweet peas are one of my favourite flowers as they smell so lovely and are well-suited to being cut and put indoors. In fact, cutting the flowers encourages the plants to keep producing. The other half (or third) of this new bed will probably be filled by my next batch of cabbages.

Day 111

The meat ration has always been a complicated one for me to work out, as it was based around 'old' money and therefore hard to translate into the modern day. Research I've done concluded that if the original meat ration of 1s 10d was given a weight equivalent, it would be around 500g today (though not including expensive cuts). With the ration now ever-decreasing, I have tried to mirror the change by reducing the total weight of meat I buy at the same proportions. Now that I have reached the stage where the ration has reduced to 1s, just over half what it was at the beginning of the war (55 per cent to be precise), I am allowing myself just 275g of meat per week.

Planning a menu with so few of the core ingredients available is becoming more challenging. I appreciate that vegetarians go without meat every day, but I am not used to being creative with vegetables and have none of the vegetarian alternatives such as soya. Almost every meat-free dish that I can manage on my rations seems to have potato as its main component. Two new dishes I will be trying this week are cheese, tomato and potato loaf, 'Lobscouse' with mash and a potato ring with seasonal vegetables.

I'm pleased that more fruit and vegetables are now becoming available, as being able to include things such as tomatoes in my diet is a great treat after several months of winter crops. The salad in my garden is ready to be eaten, along with radishes, nasturtium leaves and rocket. The tomatoes I'm growing are nowhere near ready, but local tomatoes grown under cover are on sale. Before, I was so used to eating whatever I liked all year round that I never really relished the start of new seasons. Now, I'm excited just at the thought of fresh asparagus.

Day 112

Today (Monday 23 May) is Empire Day. A holiday long-forgotten or never-known by most, Empire Day was introduced in the early 1900s, not long after the death of Queen Victoria, and celebrated the British Empire and patriotism. Traditionally, the day falls on the first Monday before 24 May, Queen Victoria's birthday. Empire Day was also celebrated in Canada and Australia.

Though the Empire is now an outdated and overly superior concept, during the years after Victoria's death it remained a deeply important thing; part of the British sense of identity. During the Second World War, this patriotism would have seemed just as precious as it had almost forty years previously. Celebrations within the community would have taken place, much as they did at other important occasions such as VE Day in 1945.

In 1958, Empire Day was renamed Commonwealth Day; a more correct post-colonial term. Though the day has largely become forgotten and goes unobserved by most in the United Kingdom, the Union Jack is still flown from many public buildings on the second Monday in May – the amended date agreed in the 1970s by participating Commonwealth countries. Commonwealth Day in 2011 was therefore officially held last week, but as I am currently in May 1941, today – the nearest Monday to the 24th – remains Empire Day in my world. In some other places, however, Commonwealth Day is held on the second Monday in March. How very confusing it all is.

Day 114

Dinner this evening was a strange dish – the wartime version of lobscouse. Lobscouse – often shortened to scouse – is a traditional meat-based stew, once popular with sailors. In Liverpool particularly, it became a common meal. The meat, often lamb or mutton, was cooked with stock and vegetables, commonly potatoes, onions and carrots. The wartime recipe bears no similarity whatsoever to this traditional meal. Instead, it is a mixture of melted butter or margarine, with grated cheese and tomatoes added. This melted cheese and tomato mix is then poured over mashed potato. I have absolutely no idea why this adaptation was given the name lobscouse, as this must have led to much disagreement and disappointment in areas where the 'real deal' was revered.

Contrary to expectations (which were not high), this was a fairly pleasant dinner. Mashed potato and tomato are not things that I would usually combine, but once the mental hurdle was passed I was able to appreciate that it was relatively tasty. I probably wouldn't wax any more lyrical about it than this, but one major point in its favour is speed – dinner was cooked and on the table in around twenty-five minutes. Not bad for a wartime recipe!

Month Five

Day 121

A bitterly disappointing day. This evening, in a fit of curiosity, I dug away at my potato plants to see how they were coming along. They've been growing like mad for weeks and are far bigger than anyone else's that I've seen, so I was very excited to see the end result. Pride does indeed come before a fall; after expectantly scraping away, ever deeper into the tyres, I came across nothing at all. Not a sausage – or rather, not a single potato. What ensued can only be described as a child's tantrum. To make matters worse, the potatoes that Ben has been growing are now all-but-ready, with plants that have grown to about a quarter of the size of mine. What on earth has gone wrong?

One possibility is that the potatoes are simply not ready yet – but the plants have finished growing and I know that the approximate right number of weeks has elapsed. I am more disappointed than I could have imagined. What's more, I was depending on eating these potatoes over the coming weeks. It's true that I can easily go out and buy some, but (as a child in a tantrum would say) 'it's not the same!' If this really were the war, the failure would be far more serious, as every bit of produce that could be grown was an essential boost to the family food supply. I'll give them a bit longer to materialise before taking the tyre towers apart in an almighty huff.

Day 126

One very positive thing that I've begun to notice is that as the number of rationed items increases, my grocery bill each week reduces. This week, I spent a third of the pre-war amount on food (just over £10 instead of £30). Most of this is spent on vegetables, as well as rationed items such as cooking fats, bacon and meat. Though I'm buying far less, I am not spending my days hungry – I simply have to be more inventive and use up all of what I buy. Vegetables, which were often the main purchase that I wasted, have become the cornerstone of every meal. My carrots no longer languish in the fridge as a testament to healthy intentions sadly thrown over for the temptation of a pizza.

Day 128

After just over four months, I'm really beginning to feel frustrated at the lack of fruit in my wartime diet. It's now June, which means that some fruits are slowly becoming available, such as local strawberries and rhubarb, but generally my life is still a fruit-free zone. Due to seasonality, the winter and spring months are naturally a fallow period, with summer and autumn proving far more plentiful. However, ordinarily I would buy imported fruit or tinned varieties; neither of which is an option now. No fruit was imported during the first few years of war and tinned fruit supplies were very limited. To make up for this, I am eating more vegetables, which doesn't seem to be quite filling the gap. When summer and autumn finally come this year, I plan to set about preserving as much fruit as possible so that during the winter I still have supplies.

Day 132

This evening, I was able to eat the first full-sized potatoes from our allotment (thank goodness I had these as a backup and wasn't relying on those from my garden). 'Knowing that the sight of peelings deeply hurts Lord Woolton's feelings', I washed them and roasted them with the skins still on. There is something very rewarding about eating something that is home-grown – particularly if you haven't grown it before.

Day 140

For lunch today I had the Oslo Meal, a dish that was heavily promoted during the war for its energy-giving qualities. Originally given to school children as an experiment, the Oslo Meal proved more successful than people expected, being credited with improving the health and development of the children.

The meal is striking in its simplicity – consisting of unlimited amounts of salad and bread and butter, with a portion of cheese and a glass of milk. The appeal for me is the ease of preparing this. Compared to most other wartime dishes, it is wonderfully quick and easy and would be good as a packed lunch for work. More surprising was how much I actually enjoyed it. It felt healthy but was also filling and kept me going for a long time. I confess, however, that the bread I ate with the meal was homemade and fresh from the oven, which was probably a little more appetising than the slices of National Loaf that most wartime people would have eaten. Never one to stray too far from the path of duty, I did honour Ministry of Food regulations and make a loaf with wholemeal flour instead of white.

Day 146

As I near the end of 1941, American food begins to become available to me. This week, I have been able to buy a tin of Spam to add to my meat ration, and cannot express how much of a treat this feels. I know that Spam is a controversial food now – some love it, while others feel much less favourably. Tinned meat goes against every food principle that the war has taught me so far – essential values such as eating fresh, seasonal and local produce. Imported and processed, this particular food goes against the grain. However, a need was felt in 1941 and tinned and dried goods met this need. I for one am not going to complain; half the delight for me lies purely in the novelty of it, as 'American supplies' present some prospect of variety in my diet.

This evening, I made Spam with leek and potato for dinner (see recipe card). Whether it's because I've been confined to a fairly restricted range of foods for a while, or because I'm getting the hang of wartime cooking, this was very well received. I ate everything, and could have eaten more if I didn't want to make my tin of meat last as long as possible. My mind spins with the possible uses for Spam: in sandwiches with watercress, in scrambled eggs, as fritters, in a pie – the list goes on. It's just a shame that after this tin is finished I'll have to wait another month before I can buy anything else. Just one tin has used my entire points ration for the month.

Day 148

Having abandoned all hope of a first early potato crop, this evening I set about digging up the plants to reuse the tyres. Last time I had an exploratory dig, there were no potatoes to be found anywhere – this time, there had been a growth spurt in the bottom tyre of my tower. Potatoes! In abundance! Well, if not in abundance, at least in existence. There are still less than I originally anticipated when planting but, having resigned myself to harvesting none at all, my little crop is especially welcome.

As if this weren't enough, my blackcurrant bush has produced its first proper yield. Picking the ripe currants, I was amazed to find the number multiplying before my eyes. After expecting a handful, I have a generous bowlful – enough for a blackcurrant pie. Not only am I delighted to have such a bounty, but this will be the first home-grown fruit of the year for me; a lovely bonus when most of my vitamins have been coming from vegetables for months.

Recipe Card: Spam with Leek and Potato

It's surprising how versatile Spam can be. Imported from America during the second half of 1941, tinned meats were a welcome supplement to the meagre meat ration. This recipe could be altered to use other kinds of tinned meat, such as corned beef, if you prefer. This recipe serves two.

Ingredients:
1 leek, chopped
Around 10 new potatoes, or equivalent chopped old potatoes
Slice of Spam around 1 inch thick, or to preference
Small amount of fat for frying
2 tsp plain flour
Half pint vegetable stock
Watercress to serve (around two handfuls)

Method:
Chop the potatoes into small pieces (halve the new potatoes if small) and boil or steam until cooked. Melt the fat in a saucepan and fry the leek until it is soft. Cut the Spam into small cubes and add to the pan, along with the cooked potatoes. Heat this through for a minute or so and then sprinkle over the flour. Add a splash of the vegetable stock and stir until the flour becomes like a paste; then slowly pour in the remainder of the stock, stirring constantly.

Cook for a few minutes, until the ingredients are in a thick sauce, and then take off the heat. Serve with a handful of watercress per person.

Recipe Card: Carrot Macaroons

These soft, light biscuits have the consistency of coconut macaroons and are very easy on the rations. Carrots were used in cooking a great deal during the war, as their natural sweetness meant less sugar could be used. This recipe will make around fifteen macaroons. They don't keep very well, so if you're cooking for a small number of people it may be wise to halve the recipe.

Ingredients:
1 small–medium carrot
6 oz/170 g self-raising flour
2 oz/55 g sugar
1 oz/25 g margarine or softened butter
A little grated chocolate (optional)

Method:
Preheat the oven to 180°C/Gas Mark 4. Put the sugar and margarine into a bowl and cream together until fluffy. Grate the carrot and stir in well. Gradually fold in the flour.

Grease a baking tray and spoon on rough dollops of mixture (around a dessertspoonful each). If you have some grated chocolate, sprinkle a small amount on the top of each dollop. Bake in the oven for around twenty minutes and cool on a wire rack before eating.

If you'd like to add a modern twist to this recipe, replace some of the grated carrot with desiccated coconut, or sprinkle coconut on the top of each macaroon before baking.

Make Do and Mend: Top Tips

How to ... darn a sock
Socks will generally wear through in the same place every time for most people. It seems a shame, however, to throw away a sock that is perfectly fine everywhere else for the sake of one hole. If you're looking to save money and material (and clothing coupons), darning is a handy skill to have in your repertoire. This can also be used to mend small holes in other items.

1 Find some thick thread or wool (depending on the thickness of your sock) in a colour that roughly matches the sock.
2 Turn the sock inside out and place something smooth and round, such as a hard ball, inside the sock, underneath the hole. This should then be stretching out the area that needs mending. If you have a darning mushroom, this will make the job easier.

---

3 Thread the needle and, beginning at one 'corner' of the hole (at the very edge of it), sew across in a straight line to make a bridge across the gap. Shift along slightly on the same side of the hole and then make another thread bridge going back the other way. Repeat this until you have a number of straight, vertical lines covering the whole of the gap.

4 It is now time to fill the gap completely by working horizontally across the threads. Once again, start in one corner of the hole and weave alternately over and under the vertical threads. When you have reached the other side, come back the other way; this time weaving under and over the opposite threads to the first time. Continue to do this, alternating which threads you pass under and over in each row, until the hole is completely covered with weaving.

5 To finish, simply pull the needle through and trim off the excess thread, leaving a little length behind for security. The tightness of your weaving should mean that the thread does not come loose. It's advisable not to tie a knot in the thread when you have finished, as this knot might be uncomfortable when wearing the sock.

How to ... make linen last longer
You may not think about your household linen in the same way that you think about clothing, but bedclothes and towels use a lot of valuable material. There are many simple ways to make this material last longer.

1 Firstly, take time every now and then to carefully check your linen for holes and tears. A tiny rip is far easier to mend than a large one. Similarly, if there are buttons, poppers or decorations attached, make sure that they are secure. Things such as these are easily lost and never replaced.

2 Wash on the minimum temperature possible and be gentle when scrubbing. Unless something is really filthy, it probably doesn't need harsh washing and a 'softly, softly' approach will help to preserve its lifespan.

---

3 Look out for thin, worn patches. On bed sheets, thin patches are most likely to be in the middle. Cutting the sheet in half lengthways and sewing together the two good outer edges will almost guarantee a few more good years.

Items Rationed by December 1941

Bacon and ham: 4 oz per week
Sugar: 10 oz per week
Cooking fats (butter, lard, margarine, etc.): 12 oz in total per week (an increase from 8 oz for winter)
Meat: to the value of 1s 2d per week, 2d of which must be corned beef
Tea: 2 oz per week
'Sweet bread spreads' (jam, syrup, treacle and marmalade): 8 oz per month
Cheese: 3 oz per week
Eggs: one egg per week
Tinned foods: 16 points per month
Milk: maximum 2 pints per week
National household milk (dried): one tin per family per month
Clothing: 66 coupons per year

In the Kitchen Garden

Things to Do:
May
This is a useful halfway point for many crops – they are not yet ready to be harvested but should be growing at a good pace. Crops such as summer/autumn cabbages can be transferred into the ground (if started off in seed trays), as can healthy-sized tomatoes, courgettes and cucumbers. Tomatoes benefit greatly from feeding, but do not feed them until they are producing flowers; if you do this before they will put too much energy into producing leaves rather than fruit.

June

During June, you should begin to appreciate the first fruits of your labour. First early potatoes could be ready for harvesting, along with early kale, peas, strawberries and – of course – salad leaves. Plant out leeks now for harvesting in autumn or winter. Purple sprouting broccoli can also be planted out now; choose a spot that you won't need to use for a while, as the plants won't be ready for harvesting until early next year. As you pick lettuce leaves, continue to sow for the next crop. If there is particularly hot weather, try sowing the seeds in a cooler spot, or in a pot that can be moved out of the sun; lettuce seeds struggle to germinate in high temperatures. Continue to plant out courgettes now.

1. German and Austrian men between the ages of sixteen and sixty were sent to internment camps for the duration of the war. (J. & C. McCutcheon Collection)

2. On 13 May 1940, troops and police began checking road-users' identification. (J. & C. McCutcheon Collection)

Left: 3. The number of weddings taking place rose dramatically in wartime, compared to the pre-war years. (Image courtesy of David Holt)

Below: 4. This photograph shows female ARP drivers sorting through the rubble of bombed-out buildings to find bedding and linen. (J. & C. McCutcheon Collection)

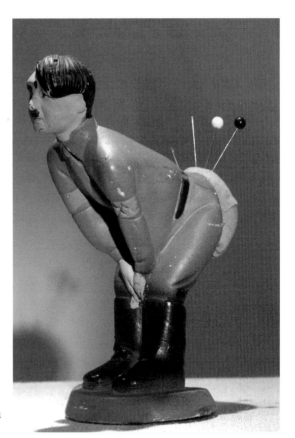

5. Allied propaganda sometimes came in the form of items and images mocking Hitler and the Nazis, to lessen the fear they induced in civilians. This pincushion, made in the United States around 1941, is a clear example of this propaganda. (Photograph by Rama, Wikimedia Commons, Cc-by-sa-2.0-fr)

6. A shopkeeper is seen stamping a ration book, having weighed out all the items. (Amberley Archive)

7. Women shelter in a tube station while their children sleep. (Amberley Archive)

8. A sign points the way to an underground shelter in London's Little Smith Street. (Image by Andrea Rota)

9. By December 1942, many items were included in the points ration, with each person having twenty points to use each month. This selection of goods, including 1 lb dried beans, dried raisins, 1 lb rice, a packet of breakfast cereal and a packet of unsweetened biscuits, would use seventeen points.

10. Other, more desirable or less available, items had far higher points values. In contrast to the decent selection of dried goods that could be bought for twenty points, a person could instead buy just one tin of American luncheon meat for the same amount.

Above: 11. A week's rations for an adult in December 1944, consisting of 2 oz cheese, 4 oz bacon, 4 oz sugar, 8 oz cooking fat, meat to the value of 1s 2d, 2 oz tea, one shell egg and 3 oz sweets or chocolate. Added to this would be twenty-four points, 2 lb jam per month, one packet of household milk per two months, two packets of dried egg per month, and a maximum of 2.5 litres of milk, depending on availability.

Left: 12. Each adult could claim 8 oz of cooking fats per week, including butter, margarine and lard. These amounts need not be equally divided between the different types of fats, though butter could only comprise 2 oz of the ration.

Right: 13. In 1944, meat could be purchased to the value of 1*s* 2*d* each week. The amount of meat that could be bought therefore depended on the type of cut and its price. Things like stewing beef could be purchased in greater quantity than more expensive meats.

Below: 14. The king and queen leave St Paul's Cathedral after the Battle of Britain thanksgiving service. (J. & C. McCutcheon Collection)

15. Two girls tend their Victory Garden. (Image courtesy of Tommy and Georgie)

16. Yellow flowers mark the beginning of a new courgette in the vegetable patch. (Image by Martin Hoy)

Opposite page:
Top left: 17. With plenty of sun, tomatoes finally begin to turn red. (Image by Andrew Fogg)

Centre: 18. Some people chose to supplement, or replace, their meagre egg ration by keeping chickens.

Top right: 19. Rhubarb flourishes on the allotment.

Bottom left: 20. If there is space, the introduction of a fruit tree to the back garden or allotment can provide a very welcome crop later on.

Bottom right: 21. A first early potato plant begins to poke its head above the soil on our allotment.

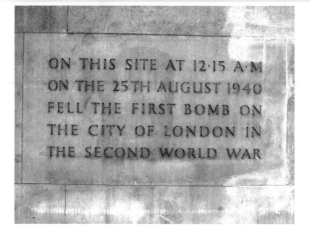

Above left: 22. A plaque marks the impact site of the first bomb to hit London, on 25 August 1940.

Above right: 23. Almost 30,000 pillboxes were built in Britain in 1940, as preparations for a possible invasion. In such an event, these would be used as local defensive positions. (Image by Graham Dean)

24. Members of the Auxiliary Fire Service putting out a fire in a bombed-out house. London suffered from repeated attacks using incendiary bombs. (J. & C. McCutcheon Collection)

25. The Home Guard played a significant role in defence. Here we see gunners manning an anti-aircraft gun on the South Coast. (J. & C. McCutcheon Collection)

26. A photograph of Winston Churchill watching anti-aircraft guns in action. (J. & C. McCutcheon Collection)

27. A view of Broadgate in Coventry before bombing began. The buildings obscuring the Cathedral were obliterated during the raids. (Image courtesy of www. historiccoventry.co.uk)

28. The smiling faces of this couple, bombed out of their house in Coventry, shows that the spirit of Britain was not easily broken. (Image courtesy of www. historiccoventry.co.uk)

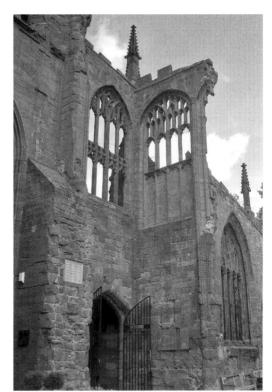

Right: 29. The damage caused to Coventry Cathedral can still be seen today. (Image by Roland Turner)

Below: 30. This photograph shows children rummaging through the rubble of their schoolroom following an air raid on Coventry. (J. & C. McCutcheon Collection)

Opposite above: 31. This group of mostly female factory workers in Yorkshire filled detonators as part of the war effort. A passenger train ran around Thorpe Arch and dropped each group of workers off at their workplaces. (Image courtesy of David Ambler)

Left: 32. A 'Keep Calm and Carry On' poster, initially designed in preparation for the invasion that never came. (Amberley Archive)

Below: 33. Women workers in a munitions factory. (Amberley Archive)

Right: 34. A young woman making brass fittings for military tanks. (Image courtesy of State Library of South Australia B 7798/425)

Below: 35. On 25 July 1940, RAF fighters brought down this German plane during a raid over the South West. (J. & C. McCutcheon Collection)

Top right: 36. Members of the Land Army at work. (Amberley Archive)

Top left: 37. Members of the Women's Land Army posted near Penzance Cornwall take some time out from their duties to pose for a photograph with local farm workers.

Left: 38. Recruitment poster published by the British Government in 1917 to encourage women to enrol with the newly created Women's Land Army. (Amberley Archive)

Bottom left: 39. Gorse in flower. It's at this time that the flowers are suitable for picking to make wine. (Image by Sean Murray)

Below: 40. The king and queen visit members of the Women's Land Army. (J. & C. McCutcheon Collection)

Top left: 41. Vine-pruning lessons for four members of the Australian Women's Land Army in 1943. (Image courtesy of State Library of South Australia B 7798/375 D. Darian Smith)

Top right: 42. A member of the Australian Women's Land Army picking grapes at Hamilton's Vineyard at Marion, South Australia, in 1943. (Image courtesy of State Library of South Australia B 7798/376 D. Darian Smith)

Bottom left: 43. Members of the Australian Women's Land Army picking an almond crop at Hamilton's Vineyard at Marion, South Australia, in 1943. (Image courtesy of State Library of South Australia B 7798/379 D. Darian Smith)

Bottom right: 44. A member of the Australian Women's Land Army milking a cow on a mixed farm at Sturt, South Australia, in 1943. (Image courtesy of State Library of South Australia B 7798/377 D. Darian Smith)

Right: 45. A member of the Australian Women's Land Army working a cultivator at Laffer's Vineyard at Sturt, South Australia, in 1943. (Image courtesy of State Library of South Australia B 7798/374 D. Darian Smith)

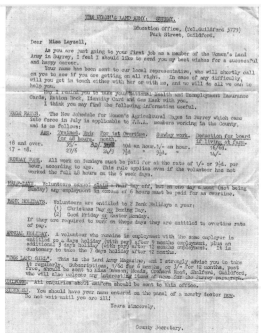

Top left: 46. Two members of the Australian Women's Land Army working with draft horses to cultivate the vines at Laffer's Vineyard at Sturt, South Australia, in 1943. (Image courtesy of State Library of South Australia B 7798/382 D. Darian Smith)

Above left: 47. A member of the Australian Women's Land Army working with a rotary hoe in a tomato crop at Hersey Brothers at Sturt, South Australia, in 1943. (Image courtesy of State Library of South Australia B 7798/381 D. Darian Smith)

Top right: 48. This letter, sent to a recently enrolled Women's Land Army member serving in Surrey, details the terms of employment. The women were worked hard, with only one week's holiday per year and a possible half-day off a week if they could be spared.

Left and bottom left: 49 & 50. These images belonged to a serving WLA worker, identity unknown, and show the lighter side of rural life.

51. An onion tentatively emerges.

52. In late April, some of the currant bushes are beginning to bear fruit.

53. In the allotment salad bed, radishes are the first to venture forth.

Centre: 54. Strawberries are grown on in small pots until they are big enough to be planted out.

55. While the leeks in my Victory Garden failed spectacularly, these ones grown on the allotment fared far better.

This page: 56., 57., 58., 59. & 60. These images belonged to a serving WLA worker, identity unknown, and show the lighter side of rural life.

61. In the garden, potatoes can be grown in stacks of tyres, whereas on the allotment there is the space for traditional banked-up beds.

62. After losing a crop of blackcurrants to the birds, a net (of somewhat hasty construction) is erected over the bush.

63. After hours of work, one of the borders is finally a suitable 'Dig for Victory' spot.

Centre: 64. Digging overgrown borders to make a vegetable patch is harder work than it seems.

65. In a garden with limited space, potatoes can be grown inside compost-filled car tyres, with more tyres needing to be added for banking up.

66. A selection of our home-made wines: sloe, peapod, gorse and apple.

67. Home-made jam, made with foraged blackberries and windfall apples from the back garden – a real wartime treat.

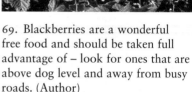

68. If the final harvest of runner beans is allowed to become mature on the plant, the seeds inside can then be taken out and dried for use the following year.

69. Blackberries are a wonderful free food and should be taken full advantage of – look for ones that are above dog level and away from busy roads. (Author)

Centre: 70. Keeping a wormery is a useful way of disposing of food and garden waste, with the added bonus of creating a fine compost and liquid fertiliser.

71. Scrap metal was very important to the war effort. Here we see the railings being removed from St James's Park. (J. & C. McCutcheon Collection)

72. After January 1942, waste rubber was called for. (J. & C. McCutcheon Collection)

Left: 73. Members of
the Home Guard stand
to attention. (Amberley
Archive)

Below: 74. The Home
Guard taking over guard
of Buckingham Palace on
14 May 1941. (J. & C.
McCutcheon Collection)

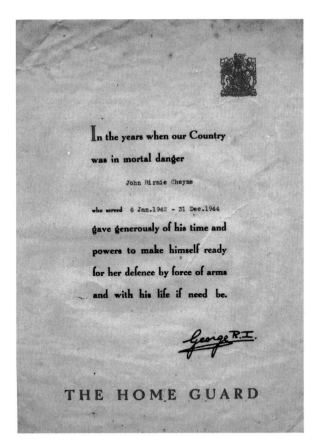

In the years when our Country
was in mortal danger

John Birnie Cheyne

who served   6 Jan.1942 - 31 Dec.1944
gave generously of his time and
powers to make himself ready
for her defence by force of arms
and with his life if need be.

George R.I.

THE HOME GUARD

Right: 75. Home Guard Commendation for John Birnie Cheyne for service between 6 January 1942 and 31 December 1944. (Image courtesy of Philippa Crabbe)

Below: 76. Workers from the United States Civilian Conservation Corps. (Image from the collection of TimothyJ)

Top: 77. Local Defence Volunteers join together for a photograph in Yorkshire. (Image courtesy of David Ambler)

Middle: 78. The Streethouse Home Guard line-up, featuring Kathleen Taylor, the only female member of the group. (Image courtesy of David Ambler)

Bottom: 79. WAAF plotters chart the movements of aircraft. (J. & C. McCutcheon Collection)

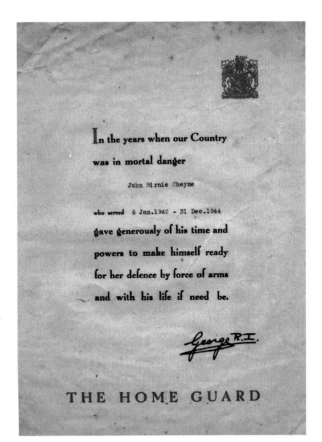

In the years when our Country
was in mortal danger

John Birnie Cheyne

who served 6 Jan.1942 - 31 Dec.1944

gave generously of his time and
powers to make himself ready
for her defence by force of arms
and with his life if need be.

George R.I.

THE HOME GUARD

Right: 75. Home Guard Commendation for John Birnie Cheyne for service between 6 January 1942 and 31 December 1944. (Image courtesy of Philippa Crabbe)

Below: 76. Workers from the United States Civilian Conservation Corps. (Image from the collection of TimothyJ)

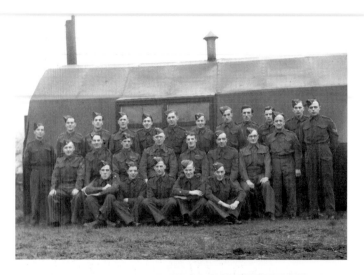

Top: 77. Local Defence Volunteers join together for a photograph in Yorkshire. (Image courtesy of David Ambler)

Middle: 78. The Streethouse Home Guard line-up, featuring Kathleen Taylor, the only female member of the group. (Image courtesy of David Ambler)

Bottom: 79. WAAF plotters chart the movements of aircraft. (J. & C. McCutcheon Collection)

Right: 80. A WAAF, Margaret Marks, poses in her wartime uniform, in around 1943. Hair was generally worn swept back away from the face for practical reasons. (Image courtesy of Roger Marks)

Below: 81. Women of the WRNS, known as Wrens, could find themselves in a variety of roles. Muriel Knight worked as a cook and was stationed in Ireland, where she met her future husband, also serving in the war. (Image courtesy of Mike and Muriel Knight)

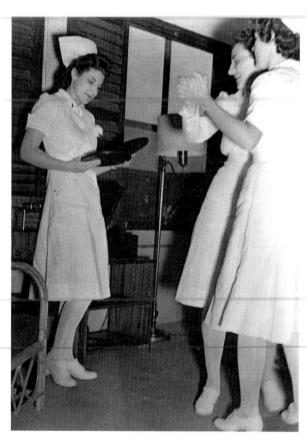

Left: 82. Nurses, probably American, take a break from duty overseas to relax and dance to some records in around 1943. (Image courtesy of John Atherton)

Below: 83. Members of the ATS learning Morse code in classroom. (Amberley Archive)

84. This memorial in Whitehall, unveiled in 2005, is dedicated to the almost 7 million women who served during the Second World War. The empty coats represent the different uniforms worn, and services entered into, by women; these include the Land Army, nursing, welding, police force and WRNS. (Image by Peep Squeak)

85. Women all over the world had to face the strain of watching their husbands, fathers and sons leave home for long periods of time with no guarantee of return. These American pilots faced the constant risk of being shot down while on duty. Some travelled to Britain to fight for the RAF before the US joined the war; the first 'Eagle Squadron' was formed in September 1940. (Image courtesy of Erin Stevenson O'Connor)

86. US soldiers in Germany at the end of the Second World War. (Image from the collection of TimothyJ)

87. US soldiers in Germany at the end of the Second World War. (Image from the collection of TimothyJ)

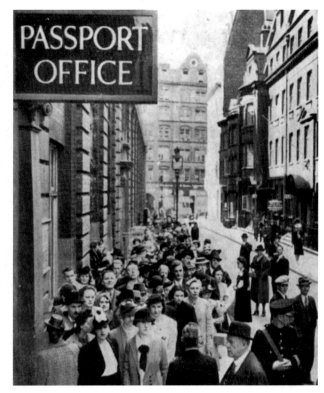

Above: 88. A blue plaque in Grove Road, East London, marks the site of the first V-1 bomb attack on the capital. (Image by Fin Fahey)

Right: 89. Parents queue to sign their children up for a scheme that evacuated children overseas. (J. & C. McCutcheon Collection)

90. A crowd outside Buckingham Palace on VE Day, greeting the king and queen. (J. & C. McCutcheon Collection)

91. A street party in full swing in Catherine Street, Swindon, in 1945. Leaning against two of the houses in the background are the large metal tops of Anderson shelters, which had been dismantled ready for collection. (Image courtesy of John Bendle)

92. A community joins together to celebrate VE Day in 1945. (Image courtesy of David Holt.)

CHAPTER FOUR: 1942

Hunger and Harvest
(July–August)

In 1942

12 January: The ration of cooking fats, which was temporarily increased, is once again reduced to 8 oz overall per week. The sugar ration is reduced from 10 oz to 8 oz. A renewed focus on the salvage of scrap metal – primarily iron and steel – leads to a patriotic drive to donate small and large quantities of metal.

25 January: Thailand declares war on the UK and USA.

9 February: The cheese ration is reduced from 3 oz per week to 2 oz per week.

14 February: In a newspaper advertisement, Cadbury announces that it has stopped making its famous milk chocolate, so that the milk may be given to children.

9 March: The points value of tinned meat and fish rises, meaning that less of these foods can be consumed. Pork sausage meat from the USA increases from eight points per lb to twelve, and USA luncheon meat increases from twelve points to twenty for 12 oz. The points cost of dried fruit and tinned and dried beans is reduced.

---

17 March: The clothing ration for the coming year is announced: the total coupons per person are reduced from sixty-six to sixty, and these coupons must now last for fourteen months instead of twelve.

April: The Women's Timber Corps (WTC) is established, recruiting women to replace men in the forestry industry. Many of those recruited come from the Women's Land Army.

6 April: Breakfast cereal and condensed milk are now included in the points rationing system, but the number of points allocated to each person rises from twenty to twenty-four per month. White bread is no longer available to buy and is instead replaced wholly by the National Loaf.

15 April: King George VI recognises the endurance of the people of Malta by awarding the 'Island Fortress of Malta' the George Cross.

28 April: The egg ration is temporarily increased from three to five eggs per person, per week.

24 June: Dried egg goes on sale, with 19,000,000 tins hitting the shelves as a first instalment.

26 July: A new rationing year begins. The points ration is once again reduced to twenty points per person, per month. Syrup and treacle are no longer counted as part of the preserves ration, but instead come under points rationing. The cheese ration is temporarily increased to 8 oz per person, per week – though despite this being announced as a short-term treat, the larger ration will remain available for almost six months.

27 July: Sweets and chocolate become rationed, at 2 oz per person, per week.

23 August: The sweets and chocolate ration temporarily increases from 2 oz per week to 4 oz, for eight weeks. After this, the ration

will change to 3 oz per week. Biscuits are added to the list of points-rationed food.

25 August: The Duke of Kent, youngest brother of King George, is killed in an air crash on a flight to Iceland.

29 August: Milk is now restricted to 3 pints per person, per week. Pregnant women, young children and some invalids are instead entitled to 1 pint a day.

28 September: Dealing with a potato glut, the government decides that the price of potatoes should be reduced to around 1*d* per lb in a bid to encourage more people to eat them instead of bread.

18 October: The points value of plain or unsweetened biscuits goes down from two points to one, per lb.

25 October: Due to a decline in milk production, the milk ration is reduced from 3 pints to 2½ per person, per week. To compensate for this, each household is entitled to a tin of dried milk every eight weeks.

1 November: New furniture is now rationed, and its purchase is restricted to newly-weds and those who have been bombed out of their homes.

15 November: Church bells ring out across the country for the first time since the outbreak of war in celebration of success in the Battle of Egypt. The sound is broadcast by the BBC in a mid-morning programme reaching the USA, South America and occupied Europe.

On 9 February 1942, soap became a rationed product. Each person was granted one soap coupon per week, which was generally given in exchange for 4 oz of household soap. Confusingly, one coupon could also be used to obtain varying weights of other kinds of soap: 3 oz of toilet soap, 3 oz of soap flakes or chips, 6 oz of soap powder No. 1, 12 oz of soap powder No. 2, or 6 oz of soft soap. Shaving soap, soap scourers, shampoo powders, liquid soap and the worryingly named dental soap were not included in the ration. Special allowance was made for miners working at collieries where there were on-site baths: here, soap was provided coupon-free. After 6 April, a second concession was made allowing mothers to buy an extra weekly ration of soap for the washing of baby clothes and linen. This extra ration applied only when a child was below one year of age.

The move to ration soap was decided upon as a way of economising with imported fats and oils, so that edible fats could be prioritised. Before this, a reported 309,000 tons of fats were being supplied to soap-makers by the Ministry of Food. Something that was now becoming common practice was the 'secret' rationing of items: to prevent a mass migration to the shops and panic-led bulk-buying, the impending soap ration was kept strictly secret until the morning of the rationing announcement. Despite this, more soap than usual had been sold in the preceding weeks – perhaps to people astute enough to realise that the restriction was coming; or to those well-connected enough to receive leaked information.

On 26 July, sweets and chocolate were added to the list of rationed items. To begin with, an 'experimental' ration was introduced, with an allowance of 2 oz per person, per week. The possibility of larger rations for children was discussed but not carried out, as it was decided that confectionery was not a necessity but a luxury. It was instead left with parents to decide whether their children should get a larger proportion of the family's combined ration. The initial ration of 2 oz was much less than the amount being produced, and less than the amount consumed by an average person each week, but as supply had become short, distribution had become uneven and unfair.

Items included in the ration were all chocolate and sweets, chewing gum and pastilles sold at chemist shops. Chocolate biscuits did not count under the new ration. As with tinned and dried goods, confectionery was obtained using coupons with a points value. These were not, however, the same kind of points coupons that were already in circulation. Coupons for sweets and chocolate had to be used separately and could not be exchanged for other points-rationed goods. Each 1 oz of confectionery counted as one point. Unlike the food-rationing system, where customers had to register with one shop and buy goods only at that place, sweet and chocolate coupons could be used at any retailers and in some cinemas.

On 23 August, the second period of chocolate rationing began, with the weekly allowance per person increasing from 2 oz to 4 oz. Each one-point coupon now allowed the buyer to obtain 2 oz of sweets or chocolate, instead of 1 oz. This doubling of the ration was only a temporary measure, however. Eight weeks later, the ration was reduced once again; this time to 3 oz per week.

As supplies of many items dwindled, prices continued to rise. War was, of course, an expensive situation, and money had to be diverted from the home front to the fight for victory. In April, as the Chancellor of the Exchequer prepared to announce the budget for the forthcoming year, it was announced that the approximate war expenditure of Britain was at £12,500,000 a day, or over £4,500,000,000 a year. This increase in taxation was not, it was argued, aimed at squeezing money out of the population, but at reducing the amount people bought. Despite an increase in tax in previous years, the amounts of leisure items such as tobacco, beer and spirits purchased had actually increased. With the budget of 1942, therefore, the Chancellor aimed to restrict buying in this sector with a further increase in taxation on the items themselves. Judging that the income of ordinary working people could not be taxed any more heavily than it was, efforts were instead made to tax their outgoings.

As a result, the duty on tobacco rose from 6½d to 7½d per ounce, with the price for ten cigarettes rising from 6½d to 9d. Purchase tax on luxury items was doubled, reaching just over 66 per cent, beer was more expensive by 2d a pint and a bottle of whisky cost 4s 8d a bottle more than it had done only days before. 'Entertainment tax', which targeted activities such as cinema and theatre trips, was doubled. The price of cinema tickets rose as a consequence, with prices now ranging from 10d for a cheap seat outside of London to 10s 6d for an expensive one in the West End: an increase of 2d.

Beauty for Duty

Despite the shortages and rationing of soap and cosmetics, during the Second World War women were expected to look their best at all times. The slogan 'beauty for duty' was adopted, and it was seen as patriotic to be well-presented. To many women, tired, busy and stressed, this must have seemed like an insult; to make matters worse, new clothes were in short supply, meaning that as the war went on everybody's pre-war clothes became shabbier. Even items that you could get new with clothing coupons were under the constraints of utility styling, and so felt dull and uniform. While hats, the mark of a well-dressed lady, did not come under rationing, they were expensive and difficult to find. Trying to become glamorous under these conditions was no joke.

Even women serving in the forces were allowed to wear make-up. The khaki uniform of the Auxiliary Territorial Service (ATS) could be complemented by a specially created Tangee lipstick. For some, livening up a drab work outfit might not have been high-priority, but for others this allowance was a real morale and confidence boost during long days spent cleaning, driving military personnel or manning (but not firing) an anti-aircraft gun. To boost the spirits of female workers in munitions factories, the Ministry of Supply issued face powder, foundation and a booklet of beauty tips. Being patriotically beautiful came at a price for the ordinary woman not in receipt of free products. Cosmetics were treated as a luxury purchase and as such were subject to incredibly high rates of taxation – when you could actually find them in the shops.

The Arrival of Uncle Sam

One exciting happening in 1942 was the arrival of American servicemen, or GIs, in the UK. To the ration-weary British public, American soldiers, with their links to products 'back home', provided a much-needed injection of glamour and fresh energy. The introduction of Americans *en masse* to reserved British society did highlight the cultural differences between the two nations, however. Americans stationed in the UK were issued with a booklet containing advice on how to behave, and introducing some of the customs that might seem unusual to them. Even fundamentals such as language were explained: instead of radios, the British had wireless sets, and instead of a railroad, a railway. Apartments were really flats, and a guinea was not actually a coin. Key messages communicated included the reassurance that the British are reserved, not unfriendly, that they dislike bragging and showing off, and that sports are popular. On the whole, communities embraced their new residents and made efforts to include them in local events and practices. Although most American units contained a chaplain, they were encouraged to attend local churches to further promote unity.

Unity was certainly something that occurred between American soldiers and the British left at home. For many women, the carefree and confident allure of the GIs was too great to resist. By the end of the war, almost 100,000 'GI Brides' had left the UK for America, accompanying their new husbands home. These love stories were not as straightforward as they might seem, however. The US government tried in vain to impose many restrictions on the marriage of its servicemen, and even after a couple wed they could face issues around European immigration. According to the Immigration Act of 1924, a maximum quota of immigrants was being enforced; a quota well below the total number of brides seeking entrance to the US. With this quota rapidly filled, many women faced the prospect of being left behind by their husbands. Realising that things must be made easier, in 1945 American powers passed Public Law 271, the War Brides Act. This Act allowed the spouses and adopted children of United States military personnel to live in the US after the war ended. In 1946, specially commissioned ships were organised to take the large numbers of brides overseas from Britain. On the whole, these women were met with excitement and curiosity from the American people; though there was resentment from a small minority who felt that the women had 'stolen their men'.

Waste Not, Want Not

The salvage of scrap metals such as iron and steel was pursued with renewed vigour during the opening months of 1942. A Director of Demolition and Recovery was appointed in January and led a sweep of the country for salvage materials. Supplies of metal from the United States had become limited due to America's own programme of production for the war. As with many things, instead of importing goods Britain needed to become self-sufficient.

A survey was carried out to gauge how much scrap metal the country had. Those owning over 3 tons of metal were required by law to disclose this to the government. The scrapping of metal railings continued at a greater pace, while other scrap such as disused rail tracks and machinery was collected. In some places, the requisitioning of railings was objected to, but those at the Ministry of Works stood their ground on what would and would not be saved. Criteria for keeping railings were defined around historic interest, artistic merit and public safety. According to the Ministry, railings dating from 1820 onwards could not generally be considered historic, and anything that could easily be copied again could not be considered of artistic value. While large items such as these were prized, it was emphasised that the everyday householder could also do their bit for national production. The smallest amounts of iron and steel might make a difference – civilians were asked to sort through their junk and domestic waste in search of old tins and nuts and bolts. A responsible citizen would then sort their household waste into different categories of salvage, much as we in the modern day sort our rubbish into different recycling bins. Tins, for instance, would be kept separate from waste paper and cardboard, which would be in a different category to rubber; separate again would be rags. Collections were then made around the country, beginning in Essex, Wiltshire and Cumberland. Collection points were set up in anticipation of this, with local groups such as the Boy Scouts helping to transport items.

It wasn't only metal that was needed, however; paper was also in short supply. Paper salvage was proceeding at an accelerated pace, and was one very clear way in which the public could contribute to the war effort. Nothing could be wasted; old books, newspapers, letters and cardboard boxes were all passed on to local authorities for recycling. Donated items were reused in the packing of munitions and were urgently needed to make shells and cartridge cases. Volunteers made house-to-house calls for the collection of suitable items. Those throwing paper into the bin were, in the eyes of most, hindering the war effort. From 9 March 1942, it was a punishable offence to burn or destroy paper or cardboard, or to dispose of it in any way other than to a collector or buyer.

A call for waste rubber was made in January 1942, after the overrunning of Malayan rubber plantations led to a major shortage. While tyres were a gratefully received addition to the rubber salvage cache, household items such as hot-water bottles and rubber sponges were equally in demand as, although smaller, the amount of reclaimable rubber was far higher. Around 30 per cent of a tyre could be used, compared to around 90 per cent of a hot-water bottle. Other items that could be used included hoses, boots, mats, aprons and soles and heels from shoes. Rubber was a much-needed material, vital for the war effort, as it was used in the manufacture of gas masks, cables, rubber boats and self-sealing petrol tanks, as well as its obvious use in tyres for military vehicles and aeroplanes. In addition to civilian salvage, the Army – one of the main beneficiaries – was also called upon to donate old tyres from vehicles to the cause. In America, boots and shoes with rubber heels made from salvage were given a 'V for Victory' mark, so that others might see their imprint across the country.

Shortages of key materials such as this meant that many brands were forced to rethink their packaging. Many products were sold in refill packaging, or customers were requested to bring their own packaging with them; paper shortages meant that most people took paper with them to the shops for their goods to be wrapped.

Baedeker Raids and 'Tip and Run' Attacks

After the Blitz of 1940 and 1941 came the Baedeker Raids of 1942. Instead of bombing sites of strategic military importance or densely populated cities, the Nazis turned their attentions to destroying Britain's historic and cultural centres. The Baedeker Raids were named after the well-known Baedeker travel guides to Britain, which it is said the Germans used when choosing their targets. Any UK city awarded three stars for its historic significance could become subject to bombing.

As with the Blitz, the Baedeker Raids were reportedly carried out as retribution for British actions. Overnight on 28 March 1942, British forces had bombed the city of Lübeck in northern Germany, causing severe damage to its historic city centre. The strength of anger at this attack came because, though Lübeck was a small port, it was an unlikely target in terms of strategic importance and was primarily a cultural destination. Fearful of plummeting morale among the people, Nazi forces exacted revenge by hitting Britain where it hurt: the country's own historic cities.

First to be bombed was Exeter, between 23–25 May. During the raids, 160,000 square miles of the city were destroyed and numerous historic buildings, including the cathedral, were damaged. Soon after came attacks on Bath, Norwich, York and Canterbury. The Bath Assembly Rooms, which in Georgian times formed the social and fashionable centre of the city, were damaged and had to undergo restoration. The harm caused, and the historic significance of various buildings in each city, was outlined in German newspapers as a boost to civilian morale. The reassuring message to the people was that for every cultural treasure the British destroyed in Germany, the Luftwaffe would hit back with vigour and precision. Every act of destruction would lead to swift retaliation.

If the Baedeker Raids weren't bad enough, the civilian population of 1942 also had to contend with the terror of 'tip and run' attacks. These raids, carried out at a low level by small, single-seat and single-engine German planes, began in March and continued until June of 1943. The campaign was carried out on the south coast of Britain, with planes flying at high speed across the Channel. German aircraft, flying low, would bomb and machine-gun towns and strategically important sites, before making an exit as rapid as their entry. The pilots chosen for this duty had to be brave and skilled fighters, as their close proximity to the towns they attacked made them especially vulnerable to British ground defences, as well as those in the air.

Even Cornwall, which had not seen particularly heavy bombing because of its rural location, came under fire during the tip and run attacks. During August, raiders sometimes came so quickly that their approach wasn't even detected. In Bodmin, nine people were killed and almost twenty injured in an afternoon raid. On the same day, two high explosives fell on a farm on the Lizard Peninsula. The audacity of these attacks shocked many; these were not night-time raids witnessed from within a dark Anderson shelter, but direct assaults carried out in broad daylight under the noses of local defence workers who didn't even see them coming. The machine-gunning of ordinary people, not planes or soldiers, was an awful prospect. Picturesque Marazion, home to the island of St Michael's Mount, was machine-gunned, and cannon fire fell on local houses. While the targets for the tip and run planes were often gas and electricity works and train lines – targets with some value to the Germans in terms of disruption – many of the missions were simply terror raids, designed to strike fear into the hearts of residential areas.

Abandoning almost all pretence of strategic importance, through the Baedeker raids and tip and run attacks of 1942, the Luftwaffe unashamedly focused on hitting the morale of those on the home front. Having only just faced up to the Blitz, it sometimes seemed that their 'keep smiling through' attitude was being tested to breaking point.

Crime and Punishment

While the Second World War is generally remembered fondly as a time when communities pulled together, widespread crime was facilitated by blackouts, air raids and restrictions. Many serving police officers went away to fight, leaving a less powerful force behind them. When war was announced, many criminals with short sentences left to serve were released from the country's prisons. The network of petty criminals was replenished but, as it would become clear, there were plenty of budding – and unlikely – miscreants on the streets of Britain's towns and cities waiting to join them. As normal life became disrupted and tensions ran high, even the most respectable people could be enticed to break the law.

However fair the rationing system was in theory, there would always be those who were keen to circumvent it. In January 1942, a man was sentenced to a month's imprisonment, with a £50 fine, for hoarding food in a bedroom. The man, an inspector with the Navy, Army and Air Force Institutes (NAAFI), which ran canteens for those serving in the forces, was said to have abused his position in order to obtain large quantities of food for personal consumption. In his home were found over 650 tins of food, including sausages, fish and soups, almost 450 bars of chocolate and 36 boxes of cheese. His sentence reflects the dim view taken of anyone who unpatriotically sought to further their own cause while others were forced to do without.

In March 1942, three officials of a local food office – one holding the rank of second in command – were sentenced to varying prison terms for receiving stolen food coupons and the theft of food coupons. One, a clerk at the food office, was sentenced to six months in prison with a £100 fine for stealing 5,000 margarine coupons. Another, also a clerk, was sentenced to nine months' imprisonment for stealing three allocations of coupons. Overall, almost 165,000 coupons were missing from their food office. Black-market coupons, as well as black-market produce, became a big problem in wartime. Illicit food coupons could be worth between £10 and £12 per thousand when sold. Petrol coupons could be sold for around two shillings per equivalent gallon of fuel. In one audacious operation in 1943, 5,225,000 clothing coupons were stolen, leaving the whole rationing system in chaos. The coupons, amounting to 299 books in six parcels, were taken from an Army Forms depot by a lieutenant and a soldier in the Royal Army Service Corps (RASC). The lieutenant was later sentenced to five years in prison, and the soldier to eighteen months.

In addition to obtaining coupons for extra items, extra items could sometimes be obtained without any coupons at all. Unscrupulous shopkeepers might keep a limited supply of black-market goods 'under the counter' for regular and trusted customers, while 'spivs' frequented local haunts with illegal supplies of cigarettes, confectionary and ladies' stockings. Some shopkeepers expected to be 'tipped' with extra money to provide customers with black-market goods. Shopkeepers that frequently allowed some customers to buy extra goods and refused to sell extra to others could face being reported by those they shunned.

There was demand for almost everything on the black market. If a product was rationed or in short supply, as most things were, somebody somewhere was bound to have it, at a price. This became such a problem that legislation was passed enabling fines of up to £500 and up to two years' imprisonment for those found guilty of supplying goods on the black market. Farmers responsible for slaughtering animals for meat were required to have a licence to do so, and could face prosecution if they slaughtered without one. Meat was a common black-market item, as it was relatively easy for farmers to kill animals without notifying the authorities, before selling the meat off the ration. In an attempt to wipe out the problem, inspectors were employed to uncover those dabbling in illegal trading. In October 1941 alone, 3,130 criminal cases were instigated by the Ministry of Food against black marketers. In January 1942, four men were sentenced to three months' hard labour for stealing and selling stockings, socks and pheasants. Newspaper accounts of this kind are numerous, and vary from minor individual cases to those concerning large businesses and seemingly respectable people. Trying to cheat rationing, or to have more than other people were able to, was condemned in the strongest possible terms by those in power. One MP described the black market as 'treason of the very worst kind.'

Looting became a major problem, with so many increased opportunities for criminals. Many houses lay empty, with mothers and children evacuated away from towns and cities, fathers and brothers sent away to war and everybody working longer hours away from home. Under the cover of the blackout, it was harder to see if a house was being looted and even harder for the police to chase a criminal. If a property was damaged by a bomb, access became easier. Some serious looters even furnished themselves with an ARP warden's helmet and arm band so that they wouldn't fall under suspicion if seen entering a building during an air raid.

Offences ranged from serious to minor but, whatever the amount or value of things taken, looting was seen as contemptible and disloyal to the country. In August 1940, an auxiliary fireman from Scotland was imprisoned for six months after stealing 100 lb of sugar from a damaged grocery store. In the same month, a waiter in London was charged with looting after taking a woollen vest and a lady's handbag from a shop. Only days later, it was reported that another Londoner had been charged with looting, stealing a jug and an alarm clock from a bombed-out house. The men were later imprisoned for twelve months and six months respectively. The crime was taken so seriously that those found guilty could, depending on the severity of their offence, face the death penalty or penal servitude.

A Message Home

During the Second World War the entire communications network owned and administered by Cable and Wireless Ltd offered its services to the British Government. The network, which connected every point within the British Empire, helped enable communication by telegram between Whitehall and the front lines, evacuees overseas and servicemen and their families. For those separated by distance and restrictions, keeping in touch had never seemed so important.

A number of schemes were implemented by Cable and Wireless for the benefit of the subjects of both Britain and the Commonwealth. These included the Expeditionary Force Message scheme, which allowed families at home to send telegrams to loved ones in the services overseas at a reduced rate and service personnel, regardless of location, to send messages home. The company also introduced a scheme where the parents or guardians of children evacuated by the Government could send one message per month, free of charge, to the evacuated child – the child's reply was also free. With these two schemes, the communications network of Cable and Wireless maintained contact between families who would otherwise have been separated during the course of the war.

Throughout the war, Cable and Wireless also provided a reduced rate for the press: 1d per word allowed correspondents in all theatres to file their reports for immediate dispatch – bringing news from the front lines to the home front on the same day. During a time of constant change and anxiety to know the latest news, such fast action was a real boost to morale.

However, when keeping in touch it was important not to give away too much. Censorship was another key function of the telegraph network during the Second World War. Messages would be censored at the point of submission – either at an overseas office, or if handed over a counter in the United Kingdom at the Central Telegraph Office, later at Electra House – Cable and Wireless headquarters in London. Messages could be censored by either trained War Office staff or seconded members of Cable and Wireless staff, in the case of some of the more remote overseas stations. Even the simplest of notes could come under careful scrutiny. Telegrams that contained any useful intelligence were handed to the Government Code and Cipher School (GC&CS) who would extract the information, censor the message, and forward it for transmission. In the case of messages from servicemen and women overseas, these messages would have any relevant tactical information removed: their location and future postings would certainly fall under the censors' pen. Those receiving messages home from a less-than-careful loved one might be confronted by little more than a card covered in black blocks.

Typical Points Values in March 1942

At this time, each person was allowed items to the value of twenty points each month. These points could either be spent on one high-value item, such as a tin of meat, or several low-value items, such as dried pulses and fruit.

USA luncheon meat (12 oz): 12–20 per can
USA luncheon meat sold sliced, or in sizes other than 12 oz: 16
Sardines: 16–24
Australian or New Zealand canned rabbit: 16
Canned crayfish, lobster and crab (per lb): 16
Canned home-produced meats (per lb): 8
Dried fruit: 6–8
Imported dried peas (per lb): 4
Canned beans in gravy: 2–4
Lentils (per lb): 2
Tapioca (per lb): 2
Whole rice (per lb): 2
Split peas (per lb): 2
Dried beans: 1–2

Items Rationed by December 1942

Bacon and ham: 4 oz per week
Sugar: 10 oz per week
Cooking fats (butter, lard, margarine, etc.): 8 oz in total per week
Meat: to the value of 1s 2d per week, 2d of which must be corned beef
Tea: 2 oz per week

Jam and marmalade: 1 lb per month
Cheese: 8 oz per week
Eggs: one per week
Sweets and chocolate: 3 oz per week
Tinned and dried foods, including breakfast cereals and biscuits: 20
    points per month
Milk: maximum 2.5 pints per week
National household milk (dried): one tin per family per two months
Clothing: 60 coupons per 14 months

Month Six

Day 162

In a strange moment of weakness, this evening I contemplated cheating and watching a television programme as a treat. Going through the options channel by channel, I could find absolutely nothing that interested me – nothing whatsoever. Programmes that I watched before the war have now begun to seem too inane and pointless; on the whole, television seems a waste of time. I enjoy watching films and am sure there will be some programming during the year that appeals to me, but I think that the break from watching television has cured me of the 'habit' of watching it. Whereas pre-war I would happily sit for whole evenings watching programme after programme, now just one hour seems too much of a waste of time.

Instead of an illicit TV treat, I settled down with the radio and my knitting and found myself to be far happier with this as a way of spending some relaxation time. It does seem strange to me that, while television seems too 'light', I am keen to listen to the radio. I'm sure the two aren't materially that different. However, with the radio on I am more likely to do other things, and feel that what I am listening to is more interesting and somehow more worthwhile as a use of my time.

I think that this differentiation is purely in my head, but I find it fascinating that after five months I have been able to rid myself of my excessive television watching. When weighing up the pros and cons of taking on the wartime lifestyle, this single sacrifice was my main reason for not wanting to go back in time. Now, I'm not that sorry to have left the television set behind. I can't wait to see if this changes when I return to modern living in seven months.

Day 166

As corned beef is now a compulsory part of the meat ration, I am faced with the problem of what to do with it. Quite honestly, before beginning this year I had never eaten corned beef; when I was a young child I found the smell of it repulsive and had managed to avoid it ever since. I do appreciate the sense in introducing corned beef to the meat ration, as the Ministry of Food's other alternative would have been simply to cut the ration even further.

My first foray into this most dreaded of foodstuffs involved cooking it on toast under a grill. This way, the fat melts, the meat sizzles and everything seems to resemble 'proper meat' a little more closely. Accompanied by a healthy dose of brown sauce, corned beef on toast is surprisingly acceptable.

Day 170

I seem to be going through a bountiful season in the victory garden and currently have vegetables aplenty. The transition from having very little produce to having a glut has passed almost imperceptibly, leaving me feeling as if I'm running to keep up. Instead of being limited to a handful of 'cold-weather veg', I am now able to enjoy fresh peas, cucumbers, marrows, kale, cabbage and the first of my runner beans. Faced with such a wealth of options, I have found myself unsure of what to do with everything. Ordinarily, I would stuff a marrow with couscous or meat in a thick tomato sauce; what on earth can one use on wartime rations?

My mother's apple tree has even decided to put on an early show this year; sitting on my dressing table is one very red, very handsome apple. While this might not seem exciting, it is my first real eating apple (as opposed to cooking apple) of the war – until now, fruit has been very scarce. Speaking of fruit; this evening I have picked a large bowl of blackcurrants from my single, once-tiny blackcurrant bush. I am extremely proud of its output. The one drawback is that the garden-netting cage we constructed around the bush made it almost as hard for me to reach the fruit as it did for the birds to.

Sticking to the principle of letting nothing go to waste, I have decided to make pea-pod wine after shelling my own weight (well, not quite) in peas. Though much-beloved in the 1970s sitcom *The Good Life*, pea-pod wine has become known for its rather potent nature and doesn't seem to be one of the 'fashionable' home-brewing choices. Nevertheless, bearing in mind the old adage 'nothing ventured ...' this evening Ben and I set about making the most of our discarded pods. These pods, boiled, cooled and with tea (for the tannins), sugar and yeast added, are now sitting in my largest pan on the dining room floor. Tomorrow this strange-smelling concoction will be transferred to a demijohn where its murky green colour can be shown off in all its glory.

Day 173

As the bounty from the garden and allotment piles up, I have begun to think more creatively about how I can use the vegetables I have a lot of. Today, I have addressed the welcome problem of having too many cucumbers. While I like cucumber, and enjoy eating it in salads, I have far more than I could eat raw (or rather, more than I could eat raw before it goes bad). As such, I have made a cucumber soup with the bulk of my glut.

Recipe Card: Cucumber Soup

This simple soup doesn't take long to cook and is a great way of using a surplus of cucumbers from the vegetable patch. For those living in the modern day, make as much as you can and freeze in portions for eating in the fallow season.

Ingredients:
2–3 medium cucumbers, or around 700–800 g
2 medium potatoes
1 large onion, finely chopped
1 oz butter
1 pint vegetable or chicken stock
2 tbsp cream or unsweetened evaporated milk (if available)
Salt and pepper to season

Method:

Chop the cucumbers in half lengthways and scoop out the seeds with a spoon. If you're keen not to waste them, set the centres aside for use in a salad. Chop the cucumbers into small pieces and dice the potatoes.

Heat the butter in a pan and fry the potato and onion for around three–four minutes. Add the chopped cucumber, season well with salt and pepper and fry for around five minutes until it begins to soften. Pour in the stock, bring to the boil and simmer for around twenty-five to thirty minutes. For a smoother consistency, mash before serving hot. If you have some, stir in the cream or evaporated milk after mashing.

Month Seven

Day 183

For the first time since beginning this experiment, I have found myself guilty of major wastage – and I couldn't feel more terrible. Having bought some lamb to make a hotpot, I became so distracted by using (and not wasting) my vegetables from the garden that I forgot all about it. Looking at it wrapped in cling film, debating whether it would still be safe to eat, I realised that I had no idea how to tell from sight if lamb has gone off. 'Smell it,' was Ben's advice. 'If lamb is off, you'll know it straight away.' How right he was. As an utterly rank odour filled my nostrils and sent me running to the bin, my heart sank. Wasting any food is awful in a wartime situation, but wasting meat is almost unforgivable. On an emotional level, I hate to think that an animal has died only to be thrown away. On a practical level, I now have no meat (aside from corned beef) for the rest of the week. With wartime rations, this makes things extremely tight.

To an outsider, my response may seem overdramatic, but I feel so awful that I could cry. The only thing that I can do now is vow never to let this happen again and to return to carefully planning my meals each day so that no food is forgotten. After being so smug about my reformed eating habits for the past few months, humble pie should certainly be on the menu for the rest of the week.

Day 191

Thanks to some good weather early on in the year, the blackberry season is beginning. At the first glimpse of a ripe blackberry I have been out scouring the hedges for fruit. So far, my hunt has only yielded a modest harvest but, coupled with some slightly ropey apples from a tree in my garden, this is enough to make a good apple and blackberry pudding. One of my favourite puddings is fruit crumble, but making the topping for a crumble can consume a fair chunk of my fats ration in one go. Alternatively, this pudding – made with breadcrumbs and just a little margarine – is a very respectable runner-up.

I am looking forward to spending the coming weeks on regular blackberry-picking walks. Again, this appeals to my newfound love of 'food for free' and makes a lovely change from the food I've been used to eating. If I can pick enough blackberries, my plan is to make jam to supplement the preserves ration and brighten up my winter menu.

Recipe Card: Baked Apple and Blackberry Pudding

This is a filling, warming dessert dish that doesn't involve sacrificing too much of your fats ration. It's also a great way of using up slightly stale bread. The blackberries could also be replaced with blackcurrants; or in the winter, raisins.

Ingredients:
Approximately 1 lb/450 g apples and blackberries
8 oz/225 g stale bread
2 oz/50 g sugar
2 oz/50 g margarine

Method:
Preheat the oven to 180°C/Gas Mark 4. Wash the blackberries thoroughly and set aside. Peel and core the apples, and slice thinly. Thoroughly break or rub the bread into breadcrumbs and mix with the sugar. Melt the margarine gently in a saucepan, remove from the heat and stir into the breadcrumbs and sugar.

Grease a pie dish and cover the bottom with a thin layer of the breadcrumb mixture. Top this with a layer of mixed fruit, and continue to layer the fruit and breadcrumbs; finishing with a layer of breadcrumbs. Bake in the oven for around forty-five minutes and serve hot.

Day 195

For dinner this evening I made baked steak, a wartime recipe in which you layer a dish with sliced potato, onion, chopped stewing steak, sausage meat and a second layer of sliced potato. This is then moistened with a mix of water, gravy powder and flour before being baked in a moderate oven. Happily, I was able to serve this with my own home-grown cabbage.

I have to say, I was initially very unsure about layering sausage meat on top of steak as the mixture of pork and beef isn't something that I've tried before. According to the recipe, the dish should be cooked for between an hour and an hour and a half, but I actually left mine in for just over two hours to allow the beef to soften a little more. The end result was very tasty, but slightly strange. I can't argue with the delicious flavour of sausage meat and potato, but I think the steak was slightly overpowered by this. Ordinarily, beef cooked in this way would be the main flavour of the meal, but it somehow got lost along the way. It surprises me that a wartime recipe such as this should include two types of meat when both aren't absolutely essential. I suspect that using sausage meat would have been seen as a way of bulking out the meagre meat ration and making a meal of this kind go further. Sausage wasn't a rationed item (although it wasn't always available), whereas steak was. Using steak alone would have made a dinner for one night, but adding sausage meat means that I have enough left over for at least one more meal; possibly two small ones. Having a dinner ready-made for tomorrow night is an added bonus when I know I'll be getting home late from work.

Day 199

Tonight, Benjamin and I went for an evening's walk/foraging expedition along the coast, looking for blackberries and sloes. It's still a bit early in the season for a blackberry glut, but there are just enough for the occasional pudding. Sloes are a fruit that I have never picked before, after the one cruel day as a child when a relative on a walk told me to 'try a wild grape' and watched as my face registered the horrendous, dry taste of the sloe.

The reason for my change of heart is that I'm keen to experiment with making sloe-based drinks. This year, aiming for a wartime-appropriate Christmas, I am planning to make as many of my gifts as possible. Sloe gin (or sloe wine, if future research shows that gin would have been hard to come by) seems a fun home-made gift that I know many of my family and friends would be open to trying. Another good motivation for the gift of sloe gin is that it needs to be made now in order to be presentable at Christmas. This means that by the start of September I will already be 'ahead of the game' in terms of Christmas planning, and will be effectively spreading the cost of this often expensive season. Hopefully, however, by making the majority of my presents I should make great strides towards lessening the financial impact of the time. How keen everyone else will be on home-made muddles remains to be seen.

Other present ideas I have had include home-made bath products (I believe you can make moisturising soaks using oats), dried herb mixes, home-made mulled apple juice and patchwork cushions.

Day 209

Yet another industrious Sunday. I have no idea why I should get so much more done on a Sunday, compared to any other day in the week, but this does seem to be the case.

This morning, I made a batch of sloe gin – which apparently entails pricking every single sloe with a fork before adding them to the gin. I bought a 70 cl bottle, and first of all decanted half into a sterilised empty wine bottle with a screw cap (a Kilner jar would work just as well). I then washed and pricked enough sloes to almost fill the empty half of the bottles once again (leaving a decent finger's-length gap at the top) before dropping them straight into the gin, one-by-one. I then added around 40 g sugar to each bottle and shook them well. In around three months, I will be able to strain this mixture through some muslin, ready to be bottled and given as gifts. Already, I can see the gin beginning to turn a nice shade of pink: a promising start. I have read of other versions of this sort of drink, instead substituting brandy for gin, or blackberries for sloes.

This afternoon, we set about gathering all the apples from the tree in my back garden. Some have begun to fall to the floor, where they rot at a rapid pace and become unusable, and I hate to feel that I am wasting food. Any apples that I could reach were picked and placed into a trug, before we were forced to fetch a ladder from the house to claim the other 98 per cent. In novels, this is the rural idyll: a warm and sunny afternoon in late summer spent gathering nature's harvest. None of these novels testify to how dangerous a sport apple-picking can be. After being struck hard on the jaw by a falling fruit while footing the ladder, I took to covering my head with my arms every time Benjamin disturbed a new branch. His cries of 'heads!' always came slightly too late to take cover, so I instead tried to listen for the ominous rustling sound of fast-descending bounty. To worsen the situation, it soon became apparent that the already rotting apples on the ground had attracted a sociable gathering of wasps, who were keen to let me know that I was on their patch.

Wasps and windfalls aside, we had soon gathered three large trugs full of apples, which are now sitting on my dining-room table. While a few are nice enough to eat as they are, most will be too sharp to eat without cooking – leaving me wondering what on earth I can do with them all. Obvious options include making pies and baked puddings. If I can pick enough blackberries over the coming week, I may also make apple and blackberry jam.

Day 210

The enemy is close at hand. In fact, it is in my back garden. Caterpillars – large, small, hairy and stripy – have invaded my vegetable patch and decimated swathes of my cabbages and kale. I neglected to check up on the Dig for Victory garden for a few days, and while I have been away these little darlings have been hard at work. I now know to my cost that I should have dedicated far more time to checking for eggs a few weeks ago; now that these eggs have hatched I am overrun with caterpillars and struggling hard to get rid of them. Some of my kale plants have been reduced to skeleton twigs in the ground, while cabbages that were almost ready are riddled with a fetching 'holey' pattern.

The first day that I spotted this carnage, I donned my gardening gloves and picked off every caterpillar that I could find. It was a long and tedious job, but afterwards I felt a sense of triumph; albeit of a 'locking the stable door after the horse has bolted' variety. This triumph has now turned to anger, however, after I ventured out into the garden this afternoon to find masses of caterpillars conjured up as if by magic. I don't want to kill them or use harsh insecticides, because I know that butterflies can be beneficial to the garden. Seeking inspiration from C. H. Middleton – the 1940s gardening guru, who gave regular radio broadcasts relating to the Dig for Victory campaign – I find that he suggests all-out war on anything that might ruin a good harvest. Growing vegetables in abundance was, after all, one of the most important duties of a home-front householder. As pretty as butterflies are, they are nonetheless seen as an enemy in our midst. His advice is to kill the butterflies before they lay eggs, kill the eggs if you're too late and pick off or kill the caterpillars if you're even later than that. I think for now I'll have to content myself with a nightly caterpillar-pick, until the problem is under control.

Day 213

I can't express how nice it has been to have an 8 oz cheese ration. Cheese is one of my favourite foods, and eating drastically less of it was a major drawback of the wartime experience for me. Since the ration has increased so much – it was at one point just 1 oz – I have been able to make so many more dishes, and manage far more easily on less meat. The sudden doubling of the ration was a result of the large amounts of dried milk and cheese imported during the first half of 1942. However, this did come at a small price; to offset the increased availability of cheese, items on the points ration became harder to obtain as the monthly points ration was reduced from twenty-four to twenty.

Making the most of the increase in cheese, over the last couple of weeks I have been making dishes such as macaroni cheese (made with dried milk instead of fresh), wholemeal cheese scones, Welsh rarebit and cheese potatoes with bacon. Cheese potatoes are a delicious and easy wartime meal (when there is enough cheese). This is simply a baked potato cooked in the oven and cut open into halves, with the filling scooped out, mashed with cheese and chopped bacon and put back inside the skins. For a nice, light meal I like it best with a home-grown summer salad. Personally, meals like this make it easy for me to forget that I'm living under rationing at all.

Recipe Card: Summer Salad

This light and easy salad was created entirely from my kitchen garden. Ingredients could be added or changed, depending on what you are growing. Other herbs that could work well are mint, coriander or chives. Quantities are kept vague so that they can be determined by individual preference or availability.

Ingredients:
Lettuce leaves
Cucumber
Nasturtium leaves
Rocket
Fresh peas, shelled but not cooked
Chopped basil
Pepper
Salt
Nut oil (I choose walnut)
Vinegar (balsamic is best, if it's the modern day)

Method:
Slice the cucumber and lay on the plate or bowl as a base for the salad. Top with the rocket, nasturtium leaves and peas, and sprinkle with chopped basil and pepper.

Make the salad dressing by mixing the nut oil and vinegar until it is to your taste. Add a pinch of salt. Depending on the strength of the vinegar you use, you may also like to add a little sugar to take away some of the acidity. Drizzle this dressing over the salad.

Serve as a side to a summer meal, such as quiche or baked fish, or with fresh bread or chopped bacon as a light lunch.

In the Kitchen Garden

Things to Do:
July
Winter may seem a long way away now, but it's already time to plant out cabbages and cauliflowers for a winter harvest. Looking ahead

even further, sow spring cabbage seeds under cover in seed trays on a windowsill or in a greenhouse. If the weather becomes very hot, take care to ventilate your greenhouse, as particularly high temperatures can prevent seed growth. Keep planting salad crops such as radishes and rocket, to prolong the harvesting period later.

August

With things still being ready for harvest, make the most of your fresh produce while you can and think about ways of storing surplus for the leaner months. Make jams with currants and berries, and pickles or chutneys with excess vegetables such as tomatoes and courgettes. Blanch and freeze vegetables such as beans, peas and courgettes. Tomatoes can be bottled in brine for later use. Don't let anything go to waste simply because you haven't got around to using it. If there is little rain, check that your plants aren't getting too dry, and water in the morning while it's cool to prevent wet leaves scorching in the sun.

Making Do
(September–October)

In 1943

1 January: Small quantities of utility furniture go on sale.

10 January: As a new rationing period begins, the cheese ration is reduced from 8 oz per person, per week, to 6 oz.

2 February: The German army surrenders at Stalingrad, in Russia; a major turning point in the war.

7 February: Tinned fruit goes on sale, with supplies of tinned English plums harvested in 1942, along with imported apricots, peaches, pears and grapefruit. The cheese ration is reduced from 6 oz to 4 oz per person, per week.

21 February: A new order comes into force which makes it an offence to wilfully destroy a milk bottle, or to retain it unreasonably.

3 March: 178 people, many of them children, are killed in a crush as they push to enter Bethnal Green Tube station during an air raid.

6 March: A 'Wings for Victory' week begins in London, with the aim of raising £150,000,000 for the Air Force.

4 April: Tinned tomatoes and tinned peas become points-rationed items, costing around six points a lb and four points a lb respectively.

20 April: In the House of Commons, it is decided that women aged eighteen to sixty-five may be called up to serve in the Home Guard. However, it is asked that preference for nomination is given to those aged over forty-five, or those not suitable for other work.

25 April: The lifting of a ban on ringing church bells is celebrated across Britain as bells ring for Easter Sunday. The BBC broadcasts the peal of York Minster Cathedral.

May: A shipment of Algerian wine arrives in Britain and is slowly distributed to shops during the following weeks; to be sold at a maximum retail price of eight shillings per bottle.

16 May: 'Operation Chastise', better known as the 'Dambusters' attack, in which an innovative bouncing bomb is used to destroy the Möhne and Edersee Dams in Germany, is carried out.

1 June: The popular film star Leslie Howard, known for his roles in *The Scarlet Pimpernel* and *The First of the Few*, is killed when the plane he is travelling on is shot down by German aircraft.

July: Actor Derrick de Marnay auctions a single banana, which sells for £5.

10 July: Allied forces invade Sicily. The island is defended by the Italian 6th Army, as well as German forces. After several weeks of fighting, full-scale withdrawal of German and Italian troops begins on 11 August.

3 September: The Allies land on the mainland of Italy, leading to an Italian surrender. An Armistice is signed between the former enemies, with the news announced on 8 September.

12 October: A large delivery of 28,000,000 lb of oranges in Britain from South Africa means that for this shipment only, every child under sixteen is able to claim between 1 lb and 2 lb depending on their age.

13 October: Italy declares war on Germany, its former ally within the Axis.

22 December: The BBC bans the broadcasting of work by writer P. G. Wodehouse after he is accused of collaboration with the Nazis for broadcasts on German radio while imprisoned there.

As the new year of 1943 began, winter and war both played a part in dampening spirits on the home front. In early January, Lord Woolton and his Ministry of Food warned the public that the coming six months would be tough, with a tightening of rations and less food available for all. Those who had been struggling to manage were told, 'The food situation is not going to be so easy in the future.' Hardships that had begun in 1942, with diminishing stocks of almost everything, seemed set to continue. In response, the Ministry called for those at home to employ yet more enterprise and ingenuity in making do with less.

Many of the constraints that civilians were to be faced with in the new year had already been introduced during the previous one: systems such as points rationing, which had spread from tinned meats and dried pulses to include breakfast cereals, syrup, treacle, biscuits and even oats – which had previously been heavily promoted as a patriotic option, due to their abundance.

Cheese was one of the few foodstuffs to be more readily available at the end of 1942 and beginning of 1943. In early January, Ministry of Food advertising urged the public to make sure they used their full 8 oz ration every week – a generous portion compared to the 2 oz per week that had been available in February 1942. However, with a tough year ahead, Lord Woolton warned, this ration was far from safe. Indeed, the cheese ration was reduced as soon as 10 January, when a new rationing period – the seventh phase of the food war – began.

At this time, it was also announced that 20 million tins of American and Canadian sardines would soon be on sale, although these would form part of the points ration at two points a tin. In February, new supplies of home-grown and lease-lend tinned fruits were also added to the points rationing system. This led to complaints from many, as the number of foods that must be bought through points seemed ever-increasing, while the number of points each person was allocated remained frozen at twenty per month. Tinned beans in gravy, which had proven so unpopular that very few people wanted to buy them, were declared points-free in order to clear unwanted stocks – a decidedly average 'bonus' in the eyes of the consumers.

In order to save on milk, household dried milk was advocated as an excellent substitute; though it failed to impress consumers, who often did not claim their full ration of it. During the opening weeks of 1943, household milk was firmly and relentlessly advertised as an excellent alternative to fresh.

Dried egg, introduced in 1942, had proven equally unpopular, though it was seen as a necessary evil by most. With shell eggs in extremely short supply, dried egg all but replaced fresh in most recipes of the time. Without it, during fallow seasons many people would have had no eggs, of any description, at all. Instead, with each person rationed to one packet of dried egg per month (approximately a dozen eggs), they could be guaranteed the equivalent of three fresh eggs per week. The unpleasant taste and texture of dried egg meant that most housewives preferred to use it in baking, though the powder could be turned into a 'fresh' egg and eaten as usual. Unless accompanied by sauce, however, this reconstituted egg did not tickle the palates of the majority on the home front. To make up a fresh egg from the dried powder, one tablespoonful of egg would be mixed with two tablespoonfuls of water to make the equivalent of one egg. The mixture, once made, did not keep well: something many people discovered to their cost.

With potatoes also in abundance, it was recommended that each person eat no less than 1 lb of them every day, with the suggestion that they be served as breakfast three times a week. Another tip for consuming your full 1 lb quota was to refuse second helpings of any food until you had eaten a second helping of potatoes. Green vegetables, such as cabbage, were another readily available healthy food. When the Ministry wasn't pushing potatoes in its advertising campaigns and information sheets, it was busy extolling the virtues of eating your greens. Cooks were advised to always shred vegetables (with a sharp knife) before cooking, to cook in a teacupful of water only, and to cook for no more than fifteen minutes to keep vitamins in. In one dramatic advertisement entitled 'Murder in the Saucepan', the Ministry outlined some of the crimes that could be committed against green vegetables, as the Vitamin C in them was killed off; actions such as soaking them in water before cooking, cooking them in a pan full of water, cooking them whole and keeping them hot for hours. With so many shortages, and hardly any fruit available, it was important that people did not diminish the vitamin content of what little fresh food they had.

In addition to the usual fluctuations in food availability, furniture was also in short supply. On 1 January, small quantities of utility furniture went on sale. Largely following the lead of utility clothing, utility furniture dealt with a shortage in materials by conforming to simple, basic designs with little embellishment. Utility items were marked with the same CC41 logo as utility clothing. Strength and durability were to be prized over fashion and beauty. Though many disliked the style of the items made, they were marginally cheaper than they would have been pre-rationing: costs had soared due to short supply and so price restrictions were implemented for the new utility products. The high numbers of people being bombed out of their homes, with their possessions lost, and an increase in marriages had contributed to a major shortage of timber by 1941.

The sale of utility furniture was restricted to newly-weds, couples expecting a baby, those who had been the victims of enemy action and any others who could show a real need. Items were sold on a principle of points rationing, with a newly married couple receiving an allowance of sixty points, later called units, with a further fifteen units for each child. Couples not furnishing a whole house would receive part-rations; for instance, twenty-five units to furnish a bedroom. In January, 7,000 permits were issued, allowing entitled people to purchase the first utility pieces. The following month, a further 11,500 were issued as supplies increased. In these early days, demand far outstripped supply and this, coupled with lazy (or overly optimistic) reading of the criteria for eligibility, meant that a large percentage of applications for permits were refused. By September, such demand led to a sharp reduction in the number of units allocated to each couple or family, with newly-weds now receiving just thirty, half the original ration, with a further seven units for each child.

To save on the time and fuel associated with transportation, a 'zoning' system was introduced, meaning that furniture was sold in the area in which it was produced. As shops often did not hold a great deal of stock, a catalogue was produced to allow buyers to browse for items. Furniture was divided into five categories: living room, bedroom, kitchen, nursery and miscellaneous (items such as bookshelves, which could go into any room). In April, an exhibition of new utility pieces was held in London to showcase the range and highlight the 'excellent taste' they demonstrated; this comment being made by a local MP opening the display.

A Design Panel was established to work on new pieces that might allow the range to continue after the war ended. Promoters of utility furniture hoped that its durability and design would lead to a more widespread distribution when materials and labour were once again in greater supply. While the principles of value for money and good quality were unanimously celebrated, utility furniture was not able to survive for long in the post-war period. New ranges were launched in 1946 and 1948, but could not keep up with competition in the marketplace and the Utility Furniture Scheme officially ended in 1952. Though many people had waxed lyrically about the design of utility furniture during the war, by the end of hostilities it had become too firmly associated with the 'make do' ethos and grim drudgery of rationing.

Typical Furniture Points Values in 1943

Bed-settee: 15
Wardrobe (4-foot): 12
Sideboard: 8
Chest of drawers (3-foot): 8

Dining table: 6
Large kitchen table: 6
Armchair: 6
Fireside chair: 5
Double bed with spring mattress: 5
Dining chair: 1
Nursery furniture: 0

Patriotism and Escapism

In the austere opening months of 1943, even big-screen entertainment
– which might have been relied upon to cheer up those on the home
front – suffered a scale-down as the government requested that the
film industry use 25 per cent less celluloid. Film studios were taken
over for use as storage space, and the number of working studios fell
dramatically. On top of this, taxes on the industry rose and staff were
called up to serve in the forces. As those in the industry discussed how
to overcome these difficulties, suggestions were made that included
reviving old films, eliminating continuous shows, and cutting down
on the number of screenings.

While the British film industry suffered, more American movies
were being made than ever before. By the beginning of 1944, the dire
state of British film was being discussed in the House of Lords, with
Lord Brabazon paying tribute to the US industry, which had risen
to the demand placed on it by consumers thirsting for new pictures.
With the output at home being so small – around 15 per cent of the
feature films produced in America – imports came to fill the cinemas,
with 80 per cent of screen time being occupied by American showings
by February 1944. A staggering 30 per cent of the money made by
the American film industry came from British screenings. Equally,
British films shown in the States drew large audiences and some, such
as *Henry V* (1944), won Oscars there.

Although film was still a relatively young trade, the switch-off of
television and general drudge of everyday life meant that more and
more people flocked to the cinema for entertainment; far more than
they do today. Escapist romantic fantasies, comedies, period pictures
and patriotic war films became hugely popular. *Casablanca*, made in

1942 and starring Humphrey Bogart and Ingrid Bergman, was one of the highest-grossing films of 1943 in America, and proved just as much a success when it began being shown in Britain in January of that year. Combining romance with a fight against the Nazis, *Casablanca* had the narrative ingredients to appeal to the interests of the masses. Other wartime hits included *Rebecca* (1940), in which Alfred Hitchcock dramatised Daphne du Maurier's dark story of jealousy, *How Green Was My Valley* (1941), a tale of a Welsh mining family at the turn of the twentieth century, and *Mrs. Miniver* (1942), starring Greer Garson as a middle-class housewife dealing with the first years of the war.

Radio is often thought of as the government's key means of communication with the public during the war. However, film also played an important role in influencing public opinion. The big screen helped to make the war seem more glamorous and patriotic, and those involved in it appear exciting and attractive. Film star David Niven, producing pictures while still engaged in military service, became the perfect, heroic RAF pilot in *The First of the Few* (1942), a picture highlighting the admirable British involvement in the war. In film, there was never any doubt that the Allies would win the war, or that their involvement in the war itself should be questioned.

Comedy, as well as war films, could carry propaganda messages. The 1940 American productions *You Nazty Spy* and *The Great Dictator* lampooned Hitler and the Nazi party. The former takes as its setting the fictional land of Moronika, where three men decide to overthrow their king and launch a dictatorship, with the comedy trio the Three Stooges taking the lead roles in the new order as 'parasite' dictators. Representing Hitler, Göring and Goebbels, the Stooges portray their characters as ridiculous, but ultimately 'defeat-able'.

The Great Dictator, starring Charlie Chaplin, depicted Hitler as Adenoid Hynkel, who persecutes Jews and dreams of becoming the ruler of the world. Due to a case of mistaken identity, a Jewish barber (also played by Chaplin) is later taken to be Hynkel and makes a speech declaring that the country should be a democracy with a 'glorious future'. The film was banned in parts of Europe, and had been refused screenings in Britain during Chamberlain's period of negotiations with Germany in pre-war 1939 (as the film was being made). However, by the time of its release in 1940 Britain welcomed

Chaplin's satire of Hitler and it drew large audiences after being premiered in London in 1941.

Music also became a popular means of bonding the home front together. Through song, artists of the day comforted those who faced separation from loved ones and assured the nation of its sense of pride and togetherness – a patriotism that would surely result in victory, if they could only grit their teeth and hold on. The now-iconic wartime song, 'We'll Meet Again', sung by Vera Lynn, was released in 1939 as many men left those at home to fight overseas. Its lyrics sum up the uncertainty and anxiety of the time, as a future meeting was by no means guaranteed, and could be far off: 'We'll meet again, don't know where, don't know when.' The words 'keep smiling through', also part of the song, became a motto for perseverance through whatever trials people might face.

The song '(There'll Be Bluebirds Over) The White Cliffs of Dover', another Vera Lynn hit, was released in 1942 as a reassurance, during the dark times of war, that peace would one day come again. Interestingly, though peace did eventually prevail, there have never actually been bluebirds over the cliffs of Dover. The song was written by two American composers – Walter Kent and Nat Burton – who chose the bluebird as its focus, despite the fact that the species is native to North America and is not found in the UK.

Vera Lynn became known as the 'Forces' Sweetheart' after being voted as British servicemen's favourite performer. During the war, she travelled to places such as Burma and Egypt to entertain the troops. In addition, she also had her own radio programme, *Sincerely Yours*, in which she passed on messages between loved ones and those in the forces.

Other performers chose to inject comedy into everyday life. The lyrics of the light-hearted song 'Run Rabbit Run' were changed to delight listeners by declaring, 'Run Adolf, run Adolf, run, run run', 'What we did once, we can do again'. Noel Coward released several wartime songs, including the comedy song 'Could You Please Oblige Us With a Bren Gun?', which showed that Britons could laugh at themselves and their own situation. The song, released in 1943, pokes fun at the shortages faced by those in the Home Guard, where weapons and supplies were scarce. Coward could also be serious when it counted – his hit 'London Pride' is an evocative and powerful tune that sums up the depth of pride in their country felt by Londoners during the time of the Blitz.

Other music became famous simply for its mass appeal and popularity at dances, which afforded a brief period of escapism. The BBC also broadcast music on the radio, although its choice tended to be firm, 'safe' family favourites such as George Formby. *Music While You Work* was a radio programme aired during the day, which played continuous music with the aim of making factory workers more motivated and productive.

Holidays at Home

With life on the home front becoming more austere every day, film was not the only escapist industry to be affected. The face of tourism also changed dramatically. People no longer had the option of 'getting away from it all' with a holiday abroad, or many miles away within Britain. Petrol shortages, train overcrowding and tighter budgets meant that all but a select or lucky few were faced with the prospect of 'holidays at home'.

The holidays at home scheme was promoted heavily by local authorities during the summer of 1941. Traditional holiday activities were set up in locations that might not usually see a holiday trade, with the aim of showing locals that they could have just as much fun at home, without having to travel to the seaside or venture abroad. In Yorkshire, the summer of 1941 saw sheepdog trials, concerts, Punch and Judy shows and cricket matches, while Huddersfield was said to have been transformed into 'an inland Blackpool', complete with six seaside donkeys.

By 1942, it had become even harder for real holidays to take place, and the Ministry of Labour and National Service was keen to throw its full weight behind the holidays at home idea. People were urged to stay home and make the most of the attractions that would be laid on for them. The government poster, displayed at train stations, asking, 'Is your journey really necessary?' reinforced the idea that leisure time away from home, however pleasant, could not be deemed essential. Towns were advised to take their summer breaks at one time, to allow for plans to be made within a specific time frame.

In London, 'play at home' holidays were set up to utilise the city's parks and green spaces, with a season of events and activities running from mid-June to September. Open-air dancing, weekend concerts, bands, fairs and children's entertainment helped to take the edge off holiday cravings. Some people chose to take working holidays instead, with inner-city factory workers volunteering to spend their free time helping gather in the harvest on farms. Those who persisted in travelling far away from home for holidays risked being seen as unpatriotic, using fuel unnecessarily and taking up room on trains that could have been occupied by those carrying out important war work. Newspaper reports were published that told of holidaymakers who had travelled away from home being caught in bombing raids and forced to help fire-fight before cutting short their trip. Instances such as these were, it was reported, a moral lesson and a reminder that the people should have taken their holiday at home.

The holidays at home scheme was seen as being so successful that by 1943 it had been made bigger and better than before. London, despite being a location much-hit by enemy attacks, became a shining example of what could be achieved within the initiative. In 1943, London County Council organised open-air opera performances as well as musical comedy, ballet, boxing tournaments and circuses. Parks and green spaces were used as much as possible, allowing people to get away from their homes and forget, however briefly, about the cares of domestic life.

The Home Guard

While many wartime forces were concerned with attacking the enemy, there was one body strictly tasked with defence. The creation of the Local Defence Volunteers (LDV), later known as the Home Guard, was set in motion in 1939, soon after the declaration of war against Germany. In the event of an invasion, which during the early years of the war was entirely probable, the Home Guard would be on hand to help fight the enemy. The force was made up of men not eligible for regular military service: those who were too old, in professions exempt from conscription or medically unfit. Though often regarded as a comedic, incompetent bunch, mocked by many, the Home Guard did provide a valuable service and recruited a remarkable number of members. Among its ranks were the entertainer George Formby, actors John Laurie and Arnold Ridley (both of whom later starred in the BBC's *Dad's Army*), and author A. A. Milne. Being part of the group allowed men at home, many of whom had fought valiantly in the First World War, to feel that they too were 'doing their bit'.

Though the feared invasion of Britain never came, some of the Home Guard really did get close to the action while serving. Members manned anti-aircraft batteries, attacking German bombers, and located enemy parachutists or those who had been shot down. In 1940, a Local Defence Volunteer captured three Luftwaffe pilots who had been brought down by anti-aircraft fire and crashed in a field. In Northern Ireland, volunteers fought against members of the IRA who were in support of the Nazis.

The Home Guard is often thought of as a distinctively male institution, populated by elderly or infirm men such as those immortalised in *Dad's Army*. However, for part of the war, there was also a female element to the service. This was a tricky situation, as the Home Guard was created to confront the threat of invasion with the potential for its members to fight. While women might have proven themselves capable of a great deal, combat remained a male-only occupation. Instead, members of the Women's Home Guard Auxiliaries carried out more traditional female roles, such as administration and communication duties. There was no official uniform for this, aside from a circular brooch bearing the initials HG.

Women's Work

Before the Second World War began, it was unusual for married middle-class women to work, as it was seen as a man's role to provide money for the family. A woman working implied that her husband's income alone was not enough to sustain the couple. Single women could, of course, quite respectably hold down a job, but were expected to relinquish their position after marriage.

The war would become a first phase in the breaking down of this system, as new opportunities were offered to women who worked.

In line with previous thinking, conscription was restricted to single women, but many married women – particularly those with no children and husbands serving overseas – chose to take up positions voluntarily. With so many men posted away from home, from the very beginning of the war there were calls for women to take up the slack and contribute just as much to the fight.

There were a number of jobs that women could do; though many weren't given the choice of signing up, there was at least variety on offer. Some women were even trained to fly aeroplanes, though they did not do so in battle. Female pilots were selected to fly aircraft such as Hurricane fighters, and later Spitfires, from the point of production to the squadrons that would ultimately be taking charge of them. As part of the Air Transport Auxiliary (ATA), they played an important part in keeping the RAF equipped. Though the women were never technically on the front line, theirs was a dangerous job – many of them, including the celebrated aviator Amy Johnson, died while on duty due to mechanical failings or adverse weather conditions.

The Women's Land Army (WLA) found women to work on farms and keep production going in the place of working men called up to fight. The WLA actually began during the First World War, when a severe shortage of men left the government and farmers with no choice but to employ women. At this time, some potential employers were unhappy with the idea of females farming and objected to their appointment.

In 1939, as war became inevitable, the scheme was revived and the government called for volunteers to join. By March, over 4,500 women had made applications; some of them from women who had previously served in the WLA in the First World War. At this point, those joining could specify whether they would like to serve in their own geographical area, or whether they were happy to be moved to where the need for them was greatest. As time went by, the need for a mobile force increased and members could find themselves posted far away from home.

Potential workers from cities were encouraged to join just as much as those who already had agricultural experience. In fact, women already employed in farming were urged not to apply, as their service was already contributing to the success of the industry. Before the war began, training was not offered to members; this would be provided only on the outbreak of hostilities. Before September 1939, anyone keen to gain skills in agriculture in preparation was instead asked to take a holiday on a farm. Just a month after war began, the WLA already numbered a force of 25,000, ready to take the places of men called up during the first round of conscription.

Though the 'Land Army Girls', as they came to be known, were not actively engaged on the front line, their service was considered absolutely essential to the war effort. It released men to fight and helped in the increased production of much-needed food as imports became more difficult. Their duties could include any kind of farm work, including harvesting hay and corn, caring for livestock, milking, lifting potatoes, planting and tractor driving.

A similarly active, outdoors role could be found within the Women's Timber Corps (WTC). Formed in 1942, the WTC sought to boost the forestry industry by replacing missing men with female recruits. Many were sourced from within the Land Army, simply transferring across, as both required the same uniform. Members of the WTC were employed in all jobs relating to forestry: felling and loading timber, driving trucks and tractors and operating sawmills.

By the end of August 1939, membership of the British Red Cross Society had increased on a nationwide scale and more than 60,000 women had declared themselves ready for auxiliary nursing work in the event of a war. Nursing was one of the few female professions to post women overseas, confronting them with the grim realities of battle. Wherever men were posted to fight, nurses were needed. Women travelled to locations including France, Hong Kong, Japan and Libya. They could find themselves attacked by enemy forces or even taken as prisoners of war.

Conscripted women could also find work in the military services within the Women's Auxiliary Air Force (WAAF), Women's Royal Naval Service (WRNS) and Auxiliary Territorial Service (ATS), the women's branch of the army. Members of the WRNS were commonly known as Wrens. Women in the services did not fight, but were recruited to roles such as cook, storekeeper, intelligence worker, radar operator, driver and electrician. A variety of women from different backgrounds could become part of the military this way. Princess Elizabeth and Winston Churchill's daughter Mary both carried out war work within the ATS.

On 11 April 1943, the queen broadcast a speech to the nation in which she praised the women of the Empire for their work during the war. They had, she said, 'earned the gratitude and admiration of all mankind'. The speech was motivated not by any special event or anniversary, but simply through the conviction that it was 'high time' that someone praised the women's dedication to the cause. Their part in the war was, Her Majesty stressed, comparable to the part played by men: 'In your different spheres, believe me, you have done all that he [man] has done in different degrees, endured all that he has endured. For you, like him, have given all that is good in you, regardless of yourself, to the same cause for which he is fighting.'

Of course, despite the hard work of women in war industries, newfound employment did not replace the work still to be done at home. While dishwashers were available in the 1930s, the majority of householders could not afford them and dishes were washed by hand. The cleaning of clothes was also done by hand. Many people, particularly the middle classes, sent their clothing out to a laundry to be washed, but as the war progressed this service was reduced and many chose to keep their washing at home. This was generally done using traditional equipment such as a dolly tub and peg, a fire-heated boiler and a mangle.

Even a supposedly simple task such as shopping was radically different, and far more time consuming, in the 1930s and 1940s. Supermarkets did not exist, so buying a range of items would involve visiting a number of different shops in the local town or village: for instance, a greengrocer, baker, butcher and fishmonger. Many shops and producers did, however, deliver their goods to the door and orders could be placed by telephone.

Items Rationed by December 1943

Bacon and ham: 4 oz per week
Sugar: 10 oz per week
Cooking fats (butter, lard, margarine, etc.): 8 oz in total per week
Meat: to the value of 1s 2d per week
Tea: 2 oz per week
Jam and marmalade: 1 lb per month

Cheese: 3 oz per week
Eggs: one per week
Sweets and chocolate: 3 oz per week
Tinned and dried foods, including breakfast cereals and biscuits: 20
  points per month
Milk: maximum 2.5 pints per week
National household milk (dried): one tin per family per two months
Clothing: 48 coupons per year

Month Eight

Day 213
Today is the first day of autumn; and what a beautiful day it has been.
The weather this morning was so nice, and so mild, that I decided to
make the most of it with a blackberry-picking walk. The lane I chose
seems to have been missed by most other blackberry pickers, and I
found no competition on my travels either. Returning home with my
horde, I found that I had enough to make blackberry and apple jam,
using some of the apples from the tree in our garden.

With some much-needed help from my mother, I have this evening
made nine pots of jam. For this, I used 2 lb of blackberries, 2 lb of
apples and 4 lb of sugar (more than six weeks' ration). Using this
much sugar was a bit painful to me, but thankfully I had a fair
amount saved up as I don't generally use sugar on a day-to-day
basis. After seeming to take ages to reach the boiling point, my jam is
now, finally, in jars and tucked away in my newly designated 'home
produce' cupboard. So far, the 'home produce' extends as far as nine
jars of jam and a fairly old jar of pickled onions.

Day 225
Dinner this evening was, yet again, a strange but tasty affair. I followed
a wartime recipe for a potato pancake: cooked potato mashed with
sausage meat, herbs and milk to make a soft mixture that can be fried.
While my so-called pancake began life quite promisingly, it wasn't
long before it had broken up and become generally quite repulsive in
appearance. By the time it came to serve up (alongside kale from my
vegetable patch), I was left with a mountain of pancake pieces. On the

plus side, however, it tasted far better than it looked and was very filling. It was also relatively quick and easy for a wartime recipe – and would be even more so if you already had potatoes cooked; perhaps left over from another meal. As I had to cook potatoes beforehand, it took slightly longer, but could nevertheless be achieved in around thirty minutes.

Day 237

After putting it off for eight months, this evening I finally made Woolton Pie for dinner. Named after Lord Woolton, the Minister for Food, the pie was created in 1941 by a chef at the Savoy Hotel, to prove that delicious and wholesome food could be made from wartime rations. The pie is essentially a base of seasonal vegetables, coated in a sauce of vegetable cooking water, vegetable extract and oats (to thicken), with either mashed potato or potato pastry on top. The official recipe, printed in *The Times* newspaper in April 1941, listed the main ingredients as 1 lb each of carrots, potatoes, swede and cauliflower, with the addition of three or four chopped spring onions. The vegetables would be diced and cooked in water, before a sauce was made with the leftover cooking water and vegetable extract. The vegetables and sauce would then be transferred into a casserole dish and the mashed potato or pastry placed on top before cooking in the oven. The pie would then be served with brown gravy. Though a recipe was published, the concept was designed to be easily altered to reflect which vegetables were available.

Woolton Pie, though widely promoted as an ideal wartime food, was not particularly well-received. In fact, it became the butt of many jokes and rhymes and has lived on in infamy ever since. Last year, before beginning this experiment, I made a Woolton Pie to test what I might be in for with regard to food during the war. That first attempt was so disgusting that it put me off trying again for this long: there was far too much topping, and the vegetables were bland and overcooked. Admittedly, each of these faults can probably be attributed to a poor cook, rather than a flawed recipe, but nevertheless the Woolton Pie got the blame in my mind.

Tonight's effort was definitely better. With autumn underway, I chose root vegetables for my pie – carrot, parsnip and swede – creating something as close as possible to the original recipe. To save on fat, I opted for a mashed potato topping instead of pastry. Though

Woolton Pie could never be described as an exciting menu choice, the result was not bad; 'not bad' being the highest accolade I can award in this case. It was filling, warming and – best of all – felt very healthy, as it is packed full of vegetables and contains very little fat. In fact, the only fat to be found in this was the small piece of butter I used in the mashed potato. One final positive comment that I could make would be that, using vegetables that are in season, Woolton Pie is a very cheap option for a family dinner. Those who like meat and rich flavours might find it lacking, however.

Recipe Card: Cheese and Bacon Potato Pie

This is a filling dish which makes the most of small cheese and bacon rations, bulking them out with lots of potato. The potato topping also means that pastry is only needed for the underside of the pie, not the top too, saving on fat.

Ingredients:
For the pastry:
5 oz/140 g flour
2½ oz/55 g fat (either the full amount in butter, or half butter and half lard)
Salt

For the pie filling:
2 medium–large potatoes
4 rashers bacon
3 oz/85 g cheese
1 tbsp chopped parsley
Salt
Pepper
Knob of butter
Dash of milk

Method:
Preheat the oven to 180°C/Gas Mark 4. In a bowl, rub together the fat and flour until the mixture resembles breadcrumbs. Season with

salt and gradually add small amounts of water until the mixture binds together. Roll out the pastry on a floured surface and use it to line the bottom of a round pie dish.

Chop the potatoes and boil in water until they are cooked. Mash well, adding a knob of butter (if it can be spared) and a little milk. Chop the bacon into fairly small pieces, place in a bowl and pour over enough boiling water to immerse. Leave the bacon in the water for two minutes and then drain. Stir the bacon into the mashed potato, along with the chopped parsley, salt, and plenty of pepper. Grate the cheese into the potato and stir well. Spoon the potato mixture into the pie dish and smooth it out with a knife or palette knife. Bake in the oven for forty to forty-five minutes until the pastry is cooked and the potato is golden.

This is a carbohydrate-heavy meal, so serve with a large green salad.

Month Nine

Day 242

I have just spent a very pleasant evening listening to the radio and knitting. It has been a surprise to me just how much I have come to rely on the radio for entertainment without television and other modern habits such as computer games. Like a wartime housewife, the radio is my main link with the 'real world' outside my front door – and, of course, the main link to an escapist world somewhere else. While those on the home front were limited to the home service and the occasional broadcasts picked up from Germany, I have a much wider choice of channels. As most everyday wartime programming is not available to listen to nowadays, I mostly tune into Radio 4, which I think offers a close comparison to the home service through its focus on current affairs and selection of radio drama. Occasionally, I switch over to Radio 3 or Classic FM for music; most probably very similar music to that broadcast during the afternoon on the home service. A typical day's schedule during the war, running from 7 a.m. to 12.15 a.m., would include news bulletins, a daily service, a selection of music, from classical pieces such as Mendelssohn to brass bands and men's choirs, fiction such as plays, short stories and serialised works (a novel by Charles Dickens, for instance), *Children's Hour*, educational talks, public announcements, such as the *Kitchen Front* cookery programme, and discussions of current affairs. Though people went to the cinema far more frequently than we do today, without television the radio (or wireless, as it was better known then) was probably the most accessed form of entertainment on a day-to-day basis.

The tales of Paul Temple, first broadcast in 1938, have become a firm radio favourite of mine from the war. A fictional amateur detective and novelist created by Francis Durbridge, Paul Temple, along with his wife Steve, seems always to find himself called upon by the police to help track down dangerous and mysterious criminals. Though many of the original broadcasts have been lost, their longevity has been rated highly enough that later recordings from the 1950s onwards have been preserved, and newer versions remade. On a gloomy autumn evening, there is no better way to pass the time than to settle down with a classic whodunnit. Perhaps the war is getting to me too much now, but this is now becoming every bit as nice as settling down in front of the television. Alternatively, perhaps I am prematurely ageing at a rapid rate.

Recipe Card: Potato Scones

These were a staple wartime dish, as they were filling and made the most of an ingredient that was in abundance: potatoes. This recipe should make enough for four people. If you have any cheese left over from the ration, grated cheese could be added to the mixture to make cheese scones. They are delicious hot from the oven, sliced in half and spread with butter.

Ingredients:
6 oz plain flour
4 oz mashed potato
1 oz cooking fat (butter, margarine or lard)
4 tbsp milk or milk and water
2 tsp baking powder
½ tsp salt
Ground black pepper (optional)

Method:

Preheat the oven to 220°C/Gas Mark 7. Mix together the flour, salt and baking powder. With the tips of your fingers, rub in the fat until the mixture resembles breadcrumbs. Add to this the mashed potato and milk and blend together until you have a soft dough; use a little more milk if it won't come together. Add in a sprinkle of black pepper if you wish to.

On a floured surface, roll out the dough to around 1.5 cm thickness and cut into small rounds with a cutter or knife. Glaze the tops with milk and place on a baking tray that is lined with greaseproof paper or well-greased. Bake in the oven for around fifteen minutes, or until lightly golden.

Day 250

With the cheese ration being cut back down to 4 oz, it feels as if 'normal' service has been resumed in terms of my wartime diet. Feeling decidedly bored with everything, this week I decided to spend some of my points allowance on some treats. Perhaps 'treats' is the wrong word; pre-war, these were items that I would buy every week. Of my twenty points for the month, I spent six on a tin of tomatoes and one on a packet of plain digestive biscuits. I like to make my own biscuits if I can, as I enjoy baking, but find that if I do this it instantly makes a large dent in my fats ration for the week. In terms of using rations to their fullest potential, it makes much more sense to spend a point on a large packet, which should last me at least two weeks, if not more.

Buying tinned tomatoes, which became part of the points ration in April 1943, really does feel like a treat. I haven't had any since I began this experiment and, strangely, during the first few weeks this was an item I really missed. In the depths of winter, limited to root vegetables, I became desperate to put a tin into my shopping basket. Having them now means that for dinner this evening I was able to make one of my all-time favourite meals: bolognese. I'm not sure how popular this would have been during the 1940s, although a *Vogue* cookery book I have, which dates back to 1939, contains a recipe for 'Italian Spaghetti' which is fairly similar; except the sauce base is one of beef stock rather than tomatoes. Nevertheless, with essential ingredients to hand – tomatoes, minced beef, garlic, herbs, onion and a small, late courgette (the last three ingredients being home-grown) – I had a meal fit for a modern-day king. My one concession to the war was the use of macaroni rather than spaghetti – this seems to feature in wartime recipes far more often and must have been a more popular, or more available, ingredient. I don't care one bit: my vitamin-C levels have been boosted and I am wonderfully full. Now, with half a tin of tomatoes left over, I can make a nice potato curry for dinner tomorrow night. This might be my best use of the points rations so far.

Day 272

Tonight's somewhat dubious gastronomic sensation came courtesy of 'haricot beef'. This is a ration-friendly dish essentially consisting of haricot beans (soaked overnight and cooked for an hour), slices of corned beef and chopped leek, layered in a dish, covered in thickened vegetable stock and baked in the oven. For the last couple of months, thoroughly sick of corned beef – which I never liked that much anyway – I have made do with a reduced meat ration by giving up my corned beef supplement. However, finding it increasingly difficult to come up with creative ways of cooking very little, this week I gave in and bought some. The one problem I found myself facing was what to do with it. Enter 'haricot beef'.

While it is not horrible, haricot beef is definitely a 'grin and bear it' sort of meal. Unusually, it actually looked better than it tasted – the gravy was too thin and watery (admittedly, my fault), the leeks were underdone and squeaky (again, probably me) and the whole thing was very unfairly weighted towards the haricot beans, which were by far the most well-represented item on the plate. Many wartime meals have surprised me by being far tastier than I thought they would be, but sadly this turned out largely as I expected. To balance out this negative feedback, I should add that it was at least filling and probably relatively healthy thanks to the beans, which are high in fibre and protein and low in fat. During the course of this experiment, I have become wonderfully adept at eating things that don't entice or excite my taste buds and clearing my plate – all except some excess gravy, which I put into the cat's bowl. He walked over, sniffed it from a distance and sauntered out into the garden. Thankfully, the dessert of apple crumble was far more interesting. My one final parting shot would be that, regardless of what any wartime food expert tries to say, corned beef will always taste like corned beef, whatever you do to it.

Recipe Card: Cocoa Cookies

These can now be made using plain flour, but during the war might have been made using 'standard' flour – National Wheatmeal flour. For a more authentically wartime result, use wholemeal flour.

Ingredients:
4 oz flour
2 oz sugar
2 oz margarine
2 tsp cocoa powder
½ tsp baking powder
5 fl. oz (¼ pint) milk
Few drops vanilla essence

Method:
Preheat the oven to 220°C/Gas Mark 7. Cream together the margarine and sugar until it is light and well-mixed. Add the vanilla essence and sift in the flour, baking powder and cocoa powder. Add the milk and mix to a soft dough. On a floured surface, roll out to half a centimetre thickness and cut into rounds or shapes. Bake on a greased or lined baking sheet for around twenty minutes and allow to cool on a wire rack.

In the Kitchen Garden

September and October are worlds apart in the kitchen garden. September was a wonderfully productive month, if not quite to the same extent as August this year. The runner-bean crop continued steadily, as did the courgettes and marrows, French beans, kale and summer cabbages.

In October, with autumn in full swing, the productivity of summer ended and I have cleared the dead plants from the vegetable patch. Even my death-defying runner beans have had their day and the bamboo canes they clambered up have been stored away for next year. With so much gone, it looks rather bare: all I have left to harvest now are parsnips, pumpkins, main-crop potatoes, kale, cabbages and different varieties of salad leaves. My tomato plants, which have done very well over the last two months, have become ropey and yellowing. Having had a good harvest of ripe tomatoes – leaving those not quite red on a windowsill to ripen fully – I decided to pick the last of them while they were still green, after a weather warning for wind and heavy rain.

While I will eat what I can from my own garden, it seems inevitable that as we head into winter I'll have to buy more vegetables from shops to supplement my home harvest. If I had better prepared myself for this, I would have planted a wider variety of winter vegetables, such as turnips, swede, carrots, cauliflowers and leeks to see me through. In fact, I did plant leeks but these turned out to be one of my main failures quite early on. The frustrating thing is that during the spring and summer, when winter vegetables would need to be planted, I did not have enough room to accommodate them anywhere; now I wish I had sacrificed some decorative, non-edible plants to fit them in.

Things to do:
September
Continue harvesting regularly – with so much ready now, crops will need checking regularly for produce as anything left on the plant too long can go off or become tough or stringy. If the weather continues fine, courgettes, beans, peas and summer cabbages should still be in full swing. Keep planting salad, such as lettuce and rocket, and keep cropping it when it is ready; this encourages them to keep growing. If you might not use it for a while, give some away.

October
As many vegetables finish cropping, clear away the old stems and begin tidying for winter. For those with a composter, old bedding plants from the garden and the remains of vegetable plants can be composted, as long as they do not have any diseases. As part of the preparations for coming months, pull out weeds and dig over the ground in your vegetable beds so that when spring comes things are in order. If you have old fallen branches or rotting pieces of trellis, chop these up and put them into bags for use as firewood over the winter.

The Final Furlong
(November–December)

In 1944

20 January: The RAF hits Berlin with 2,300 tons of bombs.

21 January: The Luftwaffe begins 'Operation Steinbock', known as the 'little blitz' or 'mini-blitz', a series of intense bombing raids over London.

17 February: The Government announces plans for the creation of a free medical service, the National Health Service, which will be introduced as soon as possible after the war.

24 March: Prisoners being held at Stalag Luft III, a prisoner of war camp 100 miles from Berlin, put into action a large-scale escape plan after digging tunnels in the sandy soil underneath the camp. Of the seventy-six people to escape, seventy-three are captured and fifty executed. This story would go on to inspire the film *The Great Escape*.

24 April: The actor and composer Ivor Novello is imprisoned for eight weeks for the misuse of petrol coupons, after receiving stolen coupons from a fan.

4 June: The Allied Fifth Army takes the previously German-held Rome and church bells ring throughout the city.

6 June: D-Day: 155,000 Allied troops land on the beaches of Normandy in France, in what is seen as the beginning of the liberation of Europe. The *Daily Telegraph* describes it as 'the greatest invasion of all time'.

10 June: Nazi soldiers massacre the village of Oradour-sur-Glane in France, after confusing it with the nearby village of Oradour-sur-Vayres, where an SS officer was said to be held by the French Resistance. 642 men, women and children are shot or burnt to death.

13 June: The first V-1 flying bomb falls on London.

20 July: Claus von Stauffenberg attempts to kill Adolf Hitler at his Wolf's Lair base in East Prussia. In 'Operation Valkyrie' Stauffenberg plants a bomb in a conference room, but Hitler survives with only a perforated eardrum.

4 August: The Jewish Frank family, including now-famous child diarist Anne Frank, are discovered hiding in a warehouse in Amsterdam by the Gestapo.

24 August: Allied forces enter Paris, finding little German resistance.

25 August: Remaining German forces in Paris surrender and Charles de Gaulle, president of the Provisional Government of the French Republic, announces the city's liberation.

7 September: Duncan Sandys, Chairman of the Flying Bomb Counter-Measures Committee, announces that 'except possibly for a last few shots, the Battle of London is over'.

8 September: A V-2 rocket hits London.

17 September: Blackout restrictions end.

---

21 October: The city of Aachen in Germany is captured by American troops.

3 December: The Home Guard stands down from duty.

15 December: A plane carrying American musician Glenn Miller vanishes while flying over the English Channel, on his way to perform in Paris. No trace of the plane or passengers is ever found.

Flying Bombs

In 1944, a new threat materialised to terrify those living on the home front. The V-1 and V-2 rockets were long-range pilotless missiles that could be launched from one country to land in another. The V-1 missile flew on autopilot and could be launched from fixed sites on the ground or from Luftwaffe planes in flight, though a launch from a fixed site was most common. Known as the 'doodlebug', it travelled at an average speed of between 300 and 350 mph and was packed with explosives, meaning that it could wipe out large residential areas in one hit. The explosive power, it was reported in June 1944, was equal to a German bomb weighing around a ton. The doodlebug was known for its distinctive engine noise, and the fact that this noise would cut out suddenly before it fell to earth. It was said that as long as you could hear the V-1, you were safe. If the noise stopped overhead, you were in trouble.

The first V-1 bomb to fall on London landed on 13 June 1944. Just before 4.30 a.m., it hit Grove Road in the east of the city, striking a railway bridge, demolishing a number of houses and killing six people. In the week that followed, newspapers were filled with details of attacks on southern England and the steps that were being taken against 'the new pilotless aircraft'. Scientists analysed the innovative weapon, producing reports to help defence officials decide how best to combat it. RAF and United States aircraft reacted quickly, attacking launch sites in Pas de Calais. Anti-aircraft guns were moved to positions outside densely populated areas, in the hope that V-1s flying overhead could be shot down before they reached large numbers of civilians. It was reported with optimism that a Spitfire had been seen shooting a V-1 out of the sky. Despite this, the menace grew.

During the weekend of 17/18 June, a massive air strike was carried out against London, killing around 200 people. Ten people were killed in Westminster, when a bomb landed in Rutherford Street. During the morning of Sunday 18 June, the Guards Chapel in St James's, home of the Royal Guardsmen at Wellington Barracks, was packed with worshippers. Just after 11 a.m., the engine of a V-1 cut out above the chapel, landing on the roof and exploding. The roof, a fairly substantial construction made of concrete, fell into the chapel, killing 121 people and injuring over 140. Rescue services worked for two days to dig out the dead and wounded.

Some areas of London were particularly vulnerable to attack. In Beckenham, twenty-two V-1s fell in June 1944 alone. Streatham was hit by twenty-nine doodlebugs in the first month of bombing, and over forty overall. Newspapers didn't devote many column inches to the death and destruction caused by these attacks, but instead tried to strike an optimistic note with repeated stories of 'overcoming the menace', reporting attacks on the Nazis' launching sites and the shooting down of projectiles. There were also thoroughly unexpected effects of flying bombs – in July a bomb fell in Camberwell, one result being that a chestnut tree was stripped of its leaves. By September, the tree had regained its foliage and, to enormous surprise, began to bloom as if spring had arrived six months early.

On 7 September, Duncan Sandys, Chairman of the Flying Bomb Counter-Measures Committee, made a statement declaring that the danger posed by V-1s had almost entirely passed, claiming, 'Except possibly for a last few shots, the Battle of London is over.' Only now that the day of the V-1 was finished did the Government seem to recognise the full extent of damage caused. A statement by Sandys at a press conference was the first full account of the fight against the flying bomb. Images were printed in newspapers, along with maps showing launch sites and vulnerable areas. During the eighty-day attack, 2,300 bombs had reached London, with alerts occurring on a regular basis and lasting for hours. One V-1 alert lasted for almost twelve hours, keeping the population in an unimaginable state of suspense. It was estimated that 92 per cent of all casualties were in the London area, with the key target and defence zone known as 'Bomb Alley'. Many had been killed and injured, but congratulations were made to those who had, Sandys thought, seen off the flying bomb. The evacuation of women and children from London and southern England was optimistically suspended, although those who had left were advised to stay away while buildings were repaired. Despite the damage caused, the weary capital breathed a sigh of relief as a period of peace seemed to lie ahead.

In one way, Sandys was right in saying that the threat had diminished. After September 1944, the V-1 became far less used as the French launch sites were taken over by Allied forces reclaiming the country. However, a new menace was on the horizon; in its place came the bigger and better V-2. Ironically, soon after Sandys made his statement, the first V-2 bombs hit London, landing in Chiswick and Epping. In Epping, there were no casualties, but in Chiswick three people were killed.

In the week beginning 25 September, eleven V-2s struck Britain. In one week in November, there were thirty-four 'incidents' relating to the rockets, with thirty-seven people reported missing as a consequence.

To begin with, despite the destruction caused, the general public wasn't told that V-2 bombs even existed. Damage was attributed to gas mains exploding, among other things. A Rocket Consequences Committee was formed in order to assess the risk of the V-2 and discuss how best to approach the crisis. In early September 1944, the committee estimated that the potential average weight of V-1 and V-2 bombs (combined) falling on London per day was 80 tons, compared to the average 48 tons of high-explosive bombs falling during the worst week of flying-bomb attacks.

As the Germans had initially said nothing about the V-2, it was felt that the British government had much to gain by also remaining silent. One reason for this was to avoid an outbreak of enemy propaganda gloating about the success of the new weapon. Another main motivation for press silence was that if reports were circulated regarding the range, success, performance and landing sites of the rockets, this information might be extremely useful to the Germans in terms of improving the weapon. While the V-2 attacks were 'hushed up', newspapers continued to report the joyous news of the end of the flying bomb, while printing mysteriously persistent and serious messages from the government, urging evacuees not to return to London. It was argued that so many houses and schools needed repair that evacuees should stay away until told to come back. Evacuations from London continued to take place and the population of the city was reduced to around 5,450,000. Only on 10 November, after two months of rocket strikes, did Winston Churchill admit to the public that Britain had been under attack. There was, he said, no need to exaggerate the danger of the V-2, as casualties and damage had so far been light. Churchill assured everyone that areas from which the rockets were being fired would soon be overrun by Allied troops. He said that, while the rockets travelled high in the sky, they fell with such a force that they burrowed deep into the ground and so actually resulted in a smaller impact zone. So powerful was the range of the V-2 that it was the first known human artefact to enter space.

Despite Churchill's reassurances, the V-2 could be highly deadly. On 25 November, a bomb fell on a busy shop in South East London, causing the deaths of 160 civilians and trapping countless others – many of them women and children – beneath the rubble. A nearby office also crumbled, leaving workers similarly entombed. A passing bus was caught in the force of the impact; the vehicle was wrecked and many of its passengers killed. Hitler wasn't finished with war-weary Britons yet.

The Home Front Overseas

It wasn't just in Britain that a home front existed. Many other countries also experienced hardships, austerity and the extra demands of war work.

Before America joined the war in 1941, it was thought of as a land of plenty in comparison to Britain, but as the war progressed American civilians also became subject to rationing. Maximum prices were set for goods to avoid excessive inflation in response to high demand. The United States introduced a rationing system in 1942, with tyres being the first item to be rationed in January. Within a year, a system similar to the one used in Britain was in place. Coupons were issued for the purchase of items such as fuel, shoes, sugar, meat, cheese, coffee and cooking fats. Even typewriters, farm equipment and stoves were rationed. Steel production was largely turned over to wartime purposes, meaning that the manufacture of machinery was limited and stocks low.

As in Britain, 'victory' recipe books were issued with revised versions of classic recipes showing how to make the best use of the weekly rations. Women were urged to use less tinned meat, to make use of fresh and perishable products such as offal and to eat more poultry and fish, which were in greater supply. While they were available, eggs and soft cheese were promoted as healthy foods to eat more of. A 1944 American information film about rationing was set in England and followed a fictional family of four to show how food and clothing rationing, including coupons and points, were managed successfully. The 'make do and mend' campaign was championed as the best way of saving clothing coupons.

Fuel for cars was issued depending on the type of driving you had to do. Non-essential driving entitled the user to 4 gallons of fuel per week and essential driving (contributing to the war effort) equated to 8 gallons. Those driving trucks delivering supplies were able to buy unlimited amounts of fuel.

The war did have some positive effects in America. Unemployment, which had been a problem pre-war, fell as wartime production resulted in the creation of new jobs. In fact, the end result was actually a labour shortage and more retired people and women, including housewives, started working. 'Rosie the Riveter' became an iconic model for women working in the factories, encouraging female pride in hard manual labour. By 1944, 20 million women worked in America, a significant increase from the 12 million working in 1940. The work was tough, however, and the pay for men and women was not often equal.

The American Women's Land Army, a part of the U.S. Crop Corps, mirrored the British Women's Land Army. Women were needed in large numbers to take the place of men called up to fight. This organisation had already worked well during the First World War and was revived once again in 1943. Alongside the Land Army ran the Victory Farm Volunteers, a body of high-school students trained to carry out farm duties to meet the need for emergency labour.

A shortage in farm workers was a problem shared by many other countries during the war. The Australian Women's Land Army (AWLA) was formed in 1942, recruiting women aged between eighteen and fifty, often from urban areas. Their duties included raising animals and assisting with growing and picking fruit and vegetables. As many were completely unskilled in farming, training was provided to teach the bare essentials.

Sharing a monarch, Australia entered the war when Britain did, on 3 September 1939. On this date, Australian Prime Minister Robert Menzies made an announcement via radio, declaring that 'in consequence of the persistence by Germany in her invasion of Poland, Great Britain has declared war upon her, and that, as a result, Australia is also at war'.

Australian forces fought for the Allies, and local defence groups were formed amid fears of an invasion. In February 1942, the country experienced its first devastating air raid when the city of Darwin, a major naval base, was bombed, killing around 250 people and wounding many hundreds more. Throughout 1942 and 1943, Australia suffered many air and sea attacks by the Japanese. Darwin was hit over sixty more times, in both civilian and military areas. Though miles away, Australians were fighting the same war as the British, and those on the Australian home front were keen to get involved to help the cause.

Those that didn't join the Women's Land Army could enlist in the Australian Women's Army Service (AWAS), Women's Auxiliary Australian Air Force (WAAAF) or Women's Royal Australian Naval Service (WRANS). Members of the AWAS were tasked with jobs that might release more men for fighting service, such as cooking, typing and driving. Some were sent overseas with the forces, to locations such as New Guinea.

Those working within the WAAAF constituted the largest female population within the women's services, with around 27,000 enlisting. The women took a variety of different roles, becoming telegraphists, electricians, flight mechanics, instrument makers and armament workers, as well as clerks, medical personnel and radar operators. Theirs could be dangerous work: fifty-seven members of the WAAAF died while on duty.

The WRANS, part of the Australian Navy, had the lowest number of female workers, though their contribution to the war was no less valiant. Initially, many were telegraphists, working with wireless technology and Morse code. Others became clerks, coders, drivers, mechanics, messengers, censors and translators.

The war impacted on so many countries and areas around the world that it is difficult to do justice to its effect on civilians. Among the Chinese there were high numbers of civilian casualties, from massacres in occupied areas to air raids, famine and biological warfare. In many countries, lack of food was a major problem. The Netherlands suffered a famine in the winter of 1944 after a German blockade prevented supplies reaching millions of people. In Poland, malnutrition was widespread as the Nazis attempted to kill the Jewish population and control the rest of the Poles through selective distribution of food. India suffered famine in 1943, resulting in the deaths of millions.

In Nazi-occupied France, civilians either accepted the new status quo and worked for the Germans, many in factories, or joined the French Resistance. Men and women in the Resistance risked their lives to undermine the occupation, sending intelligence to the Allies, launching sabotage attacks and assisting the escape of prisoners. The penalties for those caught undertaking these activities was harsh: in February 1943, the chemist France Bloch-Sérazin was decapitated in Hamburg after having been arrested, tortured and imprisoned for her role in making explosives to use against the Germans. Eighteen others were also executed for working alongside her.

German civilians also faced shortages. A rationing system similar to that used in Britain was implemented in Germany, with rationing cards required for the purchase of basic items such as meat, fats, eggs and sugar.

The Beginning of the End

At times during the war, it had seemed that the fighting, the talks and the suffering would never cease. By the end of 1944, peace was finally on the horizon. Lights went on again in London – at the end of November, Piccadilly, the Strand and Fleet Street were among the many places to be lit in the darkness for the first time since the war began. The simple fact that people could wander among the streets without the use of a blackout torch, and without fear of injuring themselves in the darkness, seemed a revelation after so many years. A *Daily Telegraph* reporter commented with surprise that he was able to read a newspaper standing underneath a street light.

With the end of the war in sight, thoughts turned to the prospect of rebuilding Britain: literally. Early on in the year, the government had begun to seriously address the shortage in housing that had resulted from the devastating effects of air raids. In some places, large numbers of houses had been destroyed or damaged to the extent that they had to be demolished. It was estimated that in Birkenhead one in twenty had been lost. In areas that had been totally devastated, the task of rebuilding actually seemed easier. If an entire street was flattened, a new one could be built from scratch in its place. However, in areas where damage was patchy, greater care had to be taken to fit in the new among the old.

In May, the first prefabricated house was built and unveiled in London. Created for demobilised troops and those who had been bombed out of their previous homes, 'prefabs' were built as a temporary solution, being placed on the site of a demolished house until a new one could be constructed. With a shortage of labour for building, it would take many years before the necessary number of houses could be erected. Some feared that temporary houses could all too easily become permanent ones, and indeed many did continue to be lived in for decades after the end of the war.

The sample prefabricated home first built for the inspection of the public was a bungalow containing two bedrooms, a living room, hall, bathroom, lavatory and kitchen. In a spirit of optimism, it was suggested that in rural areas the new houses would, in most cases, provide better living conditions than those that had been experienced before the war; though, of course, rural areas were far less likely to be in need of them than cities. Prefabrication was popular in America, as it allowed for the quick building of mass housing to address shortages. In July, an exhibition entitled 'American Housing in War and Peace' opened at the Royal Institution of British Architects, to allow the public to see how emergency housing looked. In areas that had suffered heavy bombing, such as Coventry, Swansea and Plymouth, and in busy industrial areas, plans were made for the construction of new prefabricated community centres.

On 3 December, the Home Guard held a final parade in the presence of George VI before officially standing down. Members from all over Britain and Northern Ireland joined together – some 7,000 in total – in Hyde Park to salute the king, before marching through the West End of London to be cheered by crowds. Though it was said that the Home Guard would still be on hand to respond to any emergency, from this date it ceased to exist as a body and it was generally accepted that any possible threat requiring their action had passed.

Newspapers discussing the year's activities cheerfully concluded that the German forces had ruined themselves by engaging in fighting on two fronts. It was seen to be only a matter of time before they lost, and many expected the war to be over by Christmas.

Christmas

Christmas during the war was markedly different to those that had come before. The blackout restrictions, in place for most of the years, meant that festive lights outdoors and in windows were a thing of the past. Shortages naturally had an impact on Christmas food, as many items – such as icing – were simply not available.

Despite the change in food and festivities, families who could be together at Christmas-time counted themselves lucky, as many had been split by postings overseas or evacuation. Those directly engaged in war work were urged by the Ministry of Labour to avoid slowing down production by taking just one day's holiday throughout the season – namely Christmas Day or New Year's Day.

Christmas messages could be posted to troops, but had to be sent up to three months in advance; in 1941, the deadline for post to the Middle East and India was 18 September. Numbers of people wishing to send items overseas to loved ones were so high that extra workers had to be drafted in, and additional outlets opened, to deal with the volume of mail. By the September deadline, 1,000,000 letters and cards and 80,000 parcels had been sent. While many parcels contained presents, well over half also contained Christmas pudding and cake, affording soldiers serving far away in hot climates the opportunity to remember a traditional British Advent. Many prisoners of war were supplied with Christmas parcels, containing items such as cigarettes, sweets, handkerchiefs and books.

Wherever possible, food rations were increased for the Christmas period. In 1941, extra meat, including beef and frozen Australian pork, was available. Turkeys, of which only a small number were available, were price-controlled to prevent extortionate charges, but still became an expensive option. In the same year, a double ration (12 oz) of dried fruit – including sultanas, currants, raisins, figs, apricots and apples – was available for the production of Christmas cake and pudding, or simply for a festive treat. Mincemeat was available, being included in the preserves ration (typically jam and marmalade). As shortages worsened, 'mock' alternatives to food such as turkey and goose emerged, as few families were actually able to get hold of the real thing. Mock goose was actually a mixture of potato, apple and cheese, and bore little resemblance to a pre-war feast.

The types of gifts given also changed. In 1941, a notice was issued reminding the public that 'goldsmiths are now gunsmiths': jewellers were busy contributing to the war effort by making instruments for ships, aeroplanes and armies. Jewellery would be scarce, and the range available limited. Gifts for children were naturally war-themed, including games that could be played in the blackout and army- and RAF-themed board games. Metal shortages meant that many toys for children were instead made of wood. Fewer books were available due to paper shortages, although these continued to be popular gifts. A patriotic alternative to a traditional gift was a National Savings Certificate, which allowed people to save money as they would with a bank, but with the added knowledge that the money they deposited would be used to fund wartime expenditure.

With stocks limited, buyers did their Christmas shopping very early in order to get the best items, and those who left it to November or December were advised to be happy with whatever they could get. Clothes could continue to be given as gifts, but still carried a coupon value, meaning that sending clothing to a friend meant that the giver would subsequently be forced to go without. One alternative offered by some shops was a gift-token, which would entitle the recipient to choose an item matching the value of the token, but would also require them to surrender the coupons for it themselves. There was a surge in demand for coupon-free items such as braces and suspenders.

Some large stores, such as Harrods, arranged special shopping areas where coupon-free items were arranged in one place. Within these areas were gifts such as paintings, cushions, stationery, vases and bowls. One enterprising woman sold an eggless Christmas cake recipe within a Christmas card (priced 1s) to raise money for the Red Cross and St John Fund. It was, in fact, questioned whether cards should be printed at all in a time when paper was in short supply.

Without television, community entertainment was popular and plays, pantomimes and concerts were staged by and for both children and adults. Seasonal football matches also took place, despite the fact that many players were enlisted and posted overseas. Decorations for the home tended to be fresh and natural – people collected sprigs of holly, ivy and any other available greenery to adorn walls, tables and picture frames.

The Christmas of 1944 was tough. Doodlebugs fell on Christmas Eve and, despite all hopes to the contrary, it was not all over by Christmas. There were some small consolations, however. Churches were able to have lights in their windows once again as blackout restrictions had passed, and the rations of sugar, margarine and meat were increased. To sweeten disgruntled children, there was an extra confectionery ration for the season.

Items Rationed by December 1944

Bacon and ham: 4 oz per week
Sugar: 4 oz per week
Cooking fats (butter, lard, margarine, etc.): 8 oz in total per week
Meat: to the value of 1s 2d per week
Tea: 2 oz per week (plus an extra ounce for those aged over seventy)
Jam and marmalade: 2 lb per month
Cheese: 2 oz per week
Dried egg: two packets per month
Sweets and chocolate: 3 oz per week

Tinned and dried foods, including breakfast cereals and biscuits: 24
   points per month
Milk: maximum 2.5 pints per week
National household milk (dried): one tin per family per two months
Clothing: 48 coupons per year

Month Ten

Day 279
My vegetable patch has come up trumps once again, in the (perfectly
rounded) shape of a pumpkin. Whenever I grow anything big like
this, the feeling of pride and wonder – 'I grew this!' – also increases,
compared to smaller crops. I think the pumpkin may well be my
proudest growing moment this year. After having looked at it for
days, today I finally took the difficult step of cutting into it. With it,
I made an autumnal curried pumpkin soup (see recipe card below).

Recipe Card: Curried Pumpkin Soup

If, like me, you've only ever known pumpkin to be used in pumpkin
pie at Halloween, this is a healthy alternative way of using it up. In
the 'modern day', you could stir a little cream to it before serving.

Ingredients:
1 small pumpkin
1 onion
1 clove of garlic
Around 1¼ pints/700 ml of vegetable stock or vegetable cooking
   water
2–3 heaped tsp curry powder (depending on taste)
Small knob of butter
Salt and pepper for seasoning

Method:
Hollow out the pumpkin, discarding the stringy mass in the middle,
so that you are left with firm, light flesh. If you like, the pumpkin seeds

could be toasted in a frying pan or in the oven and used as a garnish for the soup later on. Cut the soft flesh from the skin and roughly dice it into cubes of approximately 1–2 cm (I see no reason to make this a fine art).

Melt the butter in a large pan and add the onion, chopped. Cook until it begins to soften, finely chop the garlic and add this in. Cook for a further two minutes before adding the diced pumpkin. Stir in, reduce the heat slightly, cover with a lid and sweat the pumpkin for about ten minutes or until it begins to soften and break down. If it sticks to the bottom of the pan, add a very small amount of stock and cover once again. When the pumpkin has softened, add the curry powder (using less if you like a mild taste and more if you'd like a strong flavour) and let this cook in for around two minutes. Gradually add the stock or water, increasing the specified amount if you have a larger pumpkin. Do bear in mind that as the pumpkin continues to break down, the liquid in the pan will seem to increase. If in doubt, wait until the soup is almost ready and add more stock if it seems too thick – this is much easier than thickening a thin soup.

Simmer for around fifteen minutes, season with salt and pepper and then either gently mash or push through a sieve to make a smooth soup.

Day 284

Today is Armistice Day – something that I always recognise with a poppy and two minutes' silence, but something that seems slightly closer to home this year. During moments of contemplation today, I realised that I am wrong to complain about such trivial things as food and entertainment, when there were people living this lifestyle – with the added accompaniment of suffering, death, injury and sometimes a loss of home – for real. When I gripe about minor things, it is disrespectful to everyone who spent six years in a worse situation.

Day 287

I have come across an interesting news story from 1944 in an old copy of the *Daily Mail*. It was reported that the Allies had defeated a new kind of 'germ' warfare in Italy, the enemy of the moment being mosquitoes. It seems that Hitler, in a fairly ingenious plan to wipe out British and American troops travelling through Europe, as well as the Italian population, enlisted Berlin scientists to propagate the malaria virus in the insect and release it.

The newspaper reports that the scheme was thwarted by the Allies, who were given anti-malarial drugs to combat the problem. It has been more recently reported, however, that cases of malaria in Italian civilians did actually rise at the time, as locals worked in the fields and were not protected.

Day 289

Life on the home front continues quietly. It is often hard to know what to 'report' back about everyday things, as I seem to have settled into a comfortable niche of working with the rations available and adapting to the seasons. In this way, seasonally, things are always changing – sometimes, the fruit and vegetables available to me change from week to week – but in a more general sense, very little changes. I don't mean this to sound negative; it isn't a negative thing. It's just that the Second World War has started to become, well, 'normal'.

There are still days when I have the most ferocious cravings for modern food, which surprises me now as I have become used to not having things. Yesterday, it was a Pot Noodle – something I hardly ever ate, even when I had the chance to. But now that I am ten months into the experiment, I find it easier to tell myself that these are things I cannot have. Instead of railing against the wartime food, I can accept it and move on without feeling too bad about what I'm missing out on. Yes, I'd like a pizza very much, but I can't have one and there's no point wailing about that. I'm pleased that this far into my life I'm learning a bit more about self-denial.

Day 293

I have found a perfect wartime meal, and one that has been under my nose the whole time. Living in Cornwall, the Cornish pasty is a staple, classic dish – one with a long history stretching back far beyond the war. Essentially a mixture of beef, onion, potato and swede inside a pastry case, a pasty happens to be well-suited to rations. The bulk of it consists of vegetables, with the meat being just a small component. The beef used is also a relatively cheap cut – beef skirt – which would have meant that people could get more of it than they could of more expensive pieces of beef. The most potentially problematic part of a pasty in terms of rationing is the pastry, which contains butter and lard, although this uses no more fat than many wartime dishes.

Some Cornish housewives choose not to use butter, and instead use only lard. One major point in the pasty's favour, for me, is that it is an interesting way of using winter vegetables, which I can find a bit boring after a few months of eating nothing else.

Interestingly, after making pasties today I found different variations on the pasty recipe in a wartime cookery book, though none are quite the same as these traditional ones.

Recipe Card: Pasties

A traditional Cornish pasty is a wonderful thing (though, of course, being Cornish I'm biased). If you want to recreate it authentically, don't be tempted to include carrot – nice as this may potentially be, it's a giveaway marker of a non-Cornish 'Cornish' pasty. Some quantities are kept very vague as I believe it is easiest to gauge the vegetables by eye. If you chop too many vegetables or have any great amounts left over at the end, these could be made into a stew or casserole to save wasting them. This recipe makes two pasties.

Ingredients:
8 oz/225 g plain flour, or strong bread flour if you have it
2 oz/55 g butter
2 oz/55 g lard
Approx. 6 oz/170 g beef skirt
Small swede
Half a small onion
1 potato
Salt and pepper

Method:
Preheat the oven to 180°C/Gas Mark 4. Make the pastry by rubbing the butter and lard into the flour until the mixture resembles breadcrumbs. Add a little cold water and stir with a flat-bladed knife until the pastry begins to come together. Shape into a ball with your hands and chill in the fridge for at least 3–4 hours.

Finely chop the onion, and cut the beef skirt into fairly small pieces. Cut the swede into quite thin (5 mm or less) pieces around 1–1.5 cm in length (cutting the swede fairly thinly will prevent you ending up with hard, undercooked lumps of it at the end). Cut the potato in the same way.

Roll out the pastry so that it is quite thin, and cut out two round shapes using a (9-inch) 22–23 cm-diameter plate or baking dish as a guide. Keep any offcuts of pastry as these may be needed later. Lift one side of the first pastry shape and fold it over so that you are left with a semi-circle shape. Place your rolling pin at the folded edge of this semi-circle and let the pastry fall back on top of it – the rolling pin now marks the area that can be filled.

Begin by placing chopped potato on the semicircle, leaving a 1–2 cm gap all the way around the edge so that the pasty can be sealed. On top of the potato, layer swede, onion and finally beef; adding the beef last will mean that the meat juices run down over the vegetables while they cook to make a gravy. If you are unsure of how much filling to put inside the pasty, increase the quantities of vegetables slowly and carefully lift the empty half of the pastry over the top every now and then to check that the edges will still meet. When you are happy with the filling, season it well, brush around the edges of the pasty with milk and fold over the top to seal. Press down around the edges firmly and then 'patch' any holes that may have torn in the top using the leftover pastry from earlier. Using bread flour for the pastry instead of plain flour can help prevent tearing as it makes a more stretchy dough. If the pastry is tearing badly, it may simply be that the pasty has too much filling.

If you are making a real Cornish pasty, the sealed edges should now be crimped. Crimping is a hard process to describe and is far more easily understood when seen in practice. Essentially, the pastry is twisted and folded to thoroughly seal the edges, but those who aren't experts at crimping can use any other technique that works for them. The most important thing is that the curved edge of the pasty is well-sealed, which can be achieved by flattening the edges together or folding them in towards the filling. When both pasties are done this way, brush the tops with milk or egg and bake in the oven on greaseproof paper or a greased baking tray for around an hour until the pastry is golden.

Day 297

Tomorrow night, my friends Becky and Aaron are coming over for the evening and I am providing 'nibbles'. Having stupidly decided on nibbles as an alternative to dinner, I'm faced with the problem of trying to work out what on earth to make. Honestly, a full-scale dinner would probably be easier at this point as the wartime cookery books I have don't seem to be geared towards entertaining. Ordinarily, I would nip to the supermarket for pre-made fancy party food and chocolates. A wartime party isn't exactly elegant; jam tarts and fish paste sandwiches don't match up to vol-au-vents and mini gateaux. Still, in a frantic sort of way, the challenge is fun.

The element of the evening that I am really looking forward to is entertainment. I have thrown myself into the idea of creating some wartime fun and games for us all. Some of these will be actual 1940s activities, whereas others will be more retrospective. Taking advantage of modern technology to source images, I have put together a wartime picture quiz (essentially, printed sheets with pictures of wartime celebrities on, which guests have to try to identify). There'll also be era-appropriate music – and strictly no television – to create a more authentically wartime feel.

Day 298

Overall, I think that tonight's 'gathering' went well. If anything, I made too much food and am now tasked with eating it all so that it doesn't go to waste; something that I'm sure I can manage! I finally settled on an assortment of home-made nibbles, consisting of cheese straws (half the cheese ration), sausage rolls, a few nuts in shells, oven-baked crisps (courtesy of Ben) and eggless chocolate buns. Feeling very sceptical about the rising potential of the chocolate buns, I loaded each curve in the cake tin with mixture so that if they didn't rise they would still have the appearance of height. Surprisingly, the buns did rise (though not overly much), leaving me with quite a convincing plate of wartime treats. I say 'treats'; the buns, being designed to use few rations, weren't the most delicious thing I've ever made, but certainly weren't the worst either. The one criticism I'd level is that they were a bit too plain, despite the amount of cocoa in them. The addition of some chocolate chips or icing would have changed things considerably.

Day 301

As if in punishment for my smugness over the success of my vegetable patch, I today dug up my main-crop potatoes to find that the whole crop has failed. Being mindful of the first early potatoes, which I thought hadn't grown but were actually hiding deep down in the compost, at first I maintained an air of excited expectation as we removed top tyres and layers of soil. I wasn't even overly concerned as we reached the bottom tyre without disturbing a single spud, imagining that nestled at the bottom were hand-sized triumphs. Instead, to my dismay, we have unearthed seventeen so-called potatoes, fourteen of which are smaller than new potatoes and virtually inedible. Of the three slightly larger ones, none is any longer than my index finger.

The frustrating thing is that I have paid particular attention to this crop, assiduously watering in all weathers to help growth and regularly checking that there was enough soil on top. I have absolutely no idea how such a spectacular failure has happened and feel disappointed that I have spent so much time and energy when I needn't have. I can buy potatoes to eat, so it's not as if I'll starve (potatoes were sold in great quantities during wartime), but growing them myself is something that makes me feel proud, as well as saving a lot of money. Bearing in mind the amount of potatoes I eat on a daily basis, having a large crop from the garden would have been a real boon.

Day 307

Throughout the course of this year, I have been struggling to decide how to address the 'problem' of air raids. Thus far, I have shied away from attempting to replicate them, as I know that any attempt to do so would fall rather flat compared to the real thing. If I tried to create an air raid for myself, this would lack the element of surprise and would naturally happen at a time that was most convenient for me – a far cry from real air raids, which disturbed nights of sleep and wailed out in the middle of family dinners or bath times. Despite the logic behind ignoring this element of the war, I haven't been able to get away from the feeling that I am somehow cheating. When I meet up with friends and they ask how the year is going, they seem scandalised when I admit that I am not subjecting myself to this.

However, this evening the problem was taken out of my hands as I experienced my very own dash for shelter, courtesy of my friend Aaron. Being something of a technical wizard, and having heard me complain about the logistical problems of creating a bombing, he put together some sound effects and, overcoming the distance between us by making the most of the internet, styled himself as an ARP warden in a modern-day air raid.

Arriving home from work feeling tired and very hungry, I found myself hearing the distinctive siren and ran for cover under the dining room table (imagining that in a real wartime scenario this would have been a Morrison shelter). In an unheated house in the middle of winter, it wasn't hard to imagine that our dining room, being the coldest room in an old and draughty building, was as cold a shelter as a wartime equivalent may have been. Sat beneath the table, I then heard the sound of planes flying overhead and bombs dropping nearby. Though the experience could never be likened to a real one, these noises were strangely chilling and the noise of a bomb suddenly hitting the ground – or a house – made me jump more than once. So now, thanks to Aaron in his big metal hat, I have at least sat through one air raid during the course of my war. I was very glad to hear the 'all clear' and get out to make dinner at last.

Month Eleven

Day 313

Something has occurred to me that I suppose would be rather obvious if I'd ever stopped to think about it before. Since I stopped watching television on a daily basis, I've been reading far more than I ever did (even for someone who has always been a heavy reader). Because of this, I can't afford to buy books to read, even online for half their value. It just doesn't make economic sense to buy a book every week, or every other week; not to mention the fact that my already swollen bookshelves couldn't house this amount of new material.

Like many people, I've had a library card for years but never really used it and tended to buy books cheaply if I wanted something new. Since I ceased to watch television, I have been alternating between using three different libraries, depending on where I am and what

I'm doing. Obviously, the best option is the public library as this costs nothing at all and is an excellent service in terms of the sheer amount and range of books available. Better still, where I live there is a mobile library service, meaning that I needn't travel into the town to find something to read. Another real gem is a subscription library, which does involve a small outlay but provides access to an amazing number of rare, local and antiquarian books, all within an old manor house with wood-panelled walls and old-fashioned chairs and writing desks.

I'm grateful for the fact that watching less television has opened my eyes to the value of libraries. I've realised, somewhat belatedly, that if we all read more our libraries wouldn't be under threat in the way that they are now. In Cornwall, the last few years have seen the public service scaled down, with some libraries having reduced opening hours and staff being made redundant. I hope that resources such as these can be allowed to continue, somehow, into the ever-expanding digital age. What a Luddite I sound – and what a Luddite I feel at times.

Day 320

Today, we took the exciting step of opening a bottle of gorse-flower wine to try. Maybe it's just that everything tastes better in the war (less to compare it to), but it tasted delicious. In the glass, it is a very delicate pale-yellow colour, almost with the appearance of a white wine or champagne. The flavour is equally delicate and slightly floral. Our wine has ended up a little sparkling; I'm not sure if the sugar hadn't quite fermented out when we bottled it for the second time, but the sparkle was a nice surprise. When I say that we 'bottled it for the second time', I refer to a startling event that occurred a few months ago, after the wine was bottled for the first time. One evening, while standing in my kitchen, I heard a very loud bang, a crack, and felt something falling from the sky. Having no idea what was going on, I threw my hands over my face and stood as if a rabbit in the headlights. What had actually happened was that the cork from one of the wine bottles had popped out and hit the underside of a cabinet. Assuming there was simply a dodgy bottle of wine, I left it to ferment for a little longer and thought no more of it. A few days later, I heard a similar bang and a scream from the direction of the kitchen, only to find that another bottle had exploded next to my sister. However, despite the fun and games associated with home-brewing, the end result is delicious.

Day 324
With Christmas only days away, I have been busy adding the finishing touches to everything. One and a half weeks' chocolate ration is going towards my grandfather's present; I am making him chocolate truffles, which will be presented in a box I've made with some scrap cardboard decorated with wrapping paper. Aunts and uncles will be receiving home-made sloe gin and sloe vodka, which have been happily infusing away for months. Some of my other Christmas ideas – home-made bath products and mulled apple juice, for instance – haven't quite come off, but overall I'm happy with what I've produced. A sneaky success has been Ben's sloe brandy, made with cloves. It's like a deliciously strong mulled wine, and is something that will definitely be made again next year. I have bought some items, but most of these – books, theatre tickets and old-fashioned puzzle games – are still fairly 'wartime'.

Day 331
Christmas has been a thoroughly enjoyable affair, as always. This year, it was naturally a bit confused, as I tried to negotiate my way between 1944 and the present day. While I am immersed in the war, the rest of my family – despite being very supportive – would understandably be a bit dubious about a fully fledged austerity Christmas. There would be no turkey (most likely), no television, no piles of chocolate boxes – a very different occasion compared to what we are used to. As if trying to pave a way between the two options, I tried not to buy too much unnecessary food (it is only two days, after all) and to abstain as much as possible while everyone else indulged.

The result was a mixed bag of success and failure. I definitely didn't fall into the trap of spending my entire Christmas propped up in front of the television. I did succumb to one feature-length drama on Boxing Day (what a treat!), but on Christmas Day the entire family took part in an acted murder mystery game, in which we all dressed up. My costume, as a maid, was fairly easy to create using black clothing and some paper doilies as an apron and 'lacy' cap.

The whole thing was very fun and I wasn't at all sad to be missing what was on TV. I also managed to largely avoid the numerous boxes of chocolates that were passed around and I doubt I had any more than the chocolate ration would have allowed. The main treat that I well and truly cheated for was a surprise choice: tangerines. Before the war, I bought these only occasionally and would hardly ever go out of my way to have one. But now, having not had citrus fruit for almost a year, I found myself well and truly tempted by the net of fruit that arrived in our house and couldn't get enough of them. In fact, when doing the post-Christmas grocery shop I absent-mindedly picked up a net of tangerines and put it into my trolley before being reminded that I wasn't allowed them. I must also confess to having enjoyed several glasses of mulled wine and some port. I'm fairly sure that these would not have been so freely available in 1944. In fact my vodka and gin Christmas gifts probably wouldn't have been possible either, though I like to think that the thought was in the right place with these.

In the Kitchen Garden

Things to Do:
As winter comes back around, there is the opportunity to rest from garden work – though not for long. This is a perfect time to dig over empty beds and improve them for the year to come. Remove any weeds and debris, as plants such as brambles left to grow over winter will have turned into a real headache next spring. Follow this by spreading well-rotted manure or compost over the top of the plot and gently digging it into the topsoil. Bare ground can also be covered with fallen leaves to create leaf mulch and protect the soil. If you have a clay soil, take care not to dig it when it is particularly wet, as this can leave you with soil that is difficult to work with.

If you want to plant or move fruit bushes such as blackcurrant, this is the best time to do it as they now lie dormant. Apple trees and raspberry canes can be winter pruned (for raspberry pruning, see November's jobs).

One warm and cosy winter job that can be undertaken now is to sit inside with a pencil and paper and plan the vegetable garden for next year. Choose which seeds you'll need, plot out where they can be grown (making sure to rotate which crops are planted in which area each year to avoid diseases), and – if you want to be really efficient – draw up a planting calendar. When choosing crops, make sure that you factor in vegetables that can be grown for winter and spring. Summer fruit and vegetables are often so enticing that it is easy to get carried away and devote almost all the available space to them – leaving a distinct food gap later on. Planning like this may seem boring, but it will help keep the vegetable garden on track and make sure that you make the most of whatever size space you have.

November

These aren't particularly busy planting months, but during November (and December, if you live in a mild area) garlic can be planted out, as it isn't harmed by the cold. Some hardy varieties of peas can also be planted out now for a late spring (around June) crop. Plant in a sheltered spot under cloches, or make your own cloches by cutting in half 2-litre clear plastic drinks bottles and embedding the cut edges in the soil to help stop them blowing away. Broad-bean seeds can also be sown directly into the ground now.

Prune raspberries by simply cutting the main stem (the one that produced fruit this year) down to ground level and tying in any new canes that have grown out.

December

This is a good month to take hardwood cuttings from fruit bushes, if you want to try cultivating more of them. Continue harvesting winter crops such as Brussels sprouts, leeks, parsnips, winter cabbages, turnips, swedes and cauliflowers. Parsnips are hardy vegetables and can be left in the ground until you need them, although it is difficult to pull them up in frosty conditions.

Peace is Announced (January)

In 1945

20 January: The evacuation of the Auschwitz concentration camp in Poland begins.

27 January: Russian forces liberate the Auschwitz and Birkenau concentration camps. The liberation of many other Nazi camps will follow this in coming months.

4 February: The Yalta Conference begins, in which the heads of the United Kingdom, United States and Soviet Union – Winston Churchill, Franklin D. Roosevelt and Joseph Stalin – discuss the reorganisation of Europe that will take place when the war ends.

23 February: Turkey joins the war on the side of the Allies.

3 March: Finland declares war on the Axis.

4 March: Princess Elizabeth joins the Auxiliary Territorial Service (ATS) with the honorary rank of second subaltern. It is reported that she is attending a training course in driving and will receive no special privileges because of her royal status.

14 March: The RAF drops a new 22,000-lb bomb, designed by Barnes Wallis and known as the Grand Slam, on a German railway viaduct at Bielefeld.

18 March: The milk ration is increased from 2 pints to 2½ pints per week due to a rise in milk production.

19 March: Hitler issues what will become known as the 'Nero Decree', or 'scorched earth' plan, instructing that Germany's transport and communications networks, industries and military sites be destroyed before they can be taken and used by the Allies. Albert Speer, the man to whom this order is given, disobeys it.

12 April: The sudden death of US President Roosevelt is announced.

22 April: Heinrich Himmler, Hitler's Reichsführer (highest-ranking officer) of the SS, presents himself to Count Bernadotte of Sweden as the provisional ruler of Germany, stating that Hitler will soon be dead. Himmler asks Bernadotte to approach America's Dwight Eisenhower offering Germany's surrender. Hitler is furious, orders Himmler's arrest and instructs that his representative, Hermann Fegelein, be shot.

28 April: Italy's former leader Benito Mussolini and his mistress attempt to flee his country and are killed.

29 April: Hitler and Eva Braun marry in a private ceremony in Hitler's Berlin bunker.

30 April: Hitler and his new wife commit suicide in their bunker as the Red Army closes in on the centre of Berlin. According to Hitler's wishes, their bodies are burned.

1 May: Joseph Goebbels, Nazi Propaganda Minister, and his wife Magda kill their six children before committing suicide. The news of Hitler's death is broadcast by his successor, Grand Admiral Dönitz, on German radio, though the fact of his suicide is not disclosed. He

is instead said to have died in battle among the ruins of the Reich Chancellery. Initially, British newspapers also report this version of his death.

2 May: The capture of Berlin is announced by the Russian High Command. The evacuation of women and children in Britain ends.

3 May: It is reported that a captured German prisoner, Goebbels' deputy Dr Hans Fritsche, has said that Hitler committed suicide.

8 May: VE Day.

29 May: William Joyce, more commonly known as Lord Haw-Haw, the British man infamous for broadcasting Nazi propaganda since 1939, is arrested after being shot and wounded.

15 June: Joachim von Ribbentrop, former Nazi Foreign Minister, is found asleep in a flat in Hamburg and arrested.

21 July: Harry Truman, President of the United States, approves the use of an atomic bomb against Japan.

26 July: Winston Churchill resigns as Prime Minister in favour of Clement Attlee after the Conservative Party is defeated in the General Election.

6 August: Hiroshima, in Japan, is hit by a US atomic bomb.

9 August: An atomic bomb is dropped on Nagasaki.

15 August: VJ (Victory over Japan) Day: Emperor Hirohito of Japan announces his country's surrender in a radio broadcast.

2 September: Official ending of the Second World War, as the official surrender of Japan is accepted.

20 November: The Nuremberg Trials begin at Germany's Palace of
Justice. In the Trial of the Major War Criminals, twenty-four Nazis
are tried, including Hermann Göring, Karl Dönitz, Rudolf Hess
and Joachim von Ribbentrop. Of these, twelve defendants were
sentenced to death, though Göring committed suicide the night
before his execution and Martin Bormann was not at the trials.

The year 1945 began as a bleak period in the history of the war.
There were no great disasters on the scale of the Blitz, but the hope of
peace that had dawned at the end of the previous year now seemed to
burn out. Very little happened, and civilians faced a cold, grey winter
and the prospect of continuing drudgery. In a New Year broadcast,
Hitler declared that Germany would never negotiate on its surrender,
and that the war would not be over before 1946.

Nevertheless, slowly but surely, progress was made. Those on the
home front heard how Warsaw, the German-occupied Polish capital,
was taken by Russian and Polish troops in a series of Soviet victories
that a Moscow radio station described as 'the victory march to
Berlin'. In February, Churchill, President Roosevelt and Joseph Stalin
attended the Yalta Conference, or Crimea Conference, to discuss the
occupation of Germany after Hitler's defeat and an agreement for
enforcing his unconditional surrender.

Only a day later, British and American bombing raids on the
German city of Dresden began, in addition to raids on Magdeburg,
Bonn and Nuremberg. Almost 4,000 tons of bombs were dropped on
Dresden, destroying 15 square miles of the city centre and killing and
injuring large numbers. A newspaper report at the time estimated that,
instead of Dresden's usual population of 640,000, up to 2,000,000
people were actually present during the raids, as many had fled there
from the east and Berlin and troops were also in place. Estimates
of the death count varied wildly, but it is now thought that around
25,000 died between 13 and 15 February. As the city was engulfed
by a tremendous firestorm, some victims collapsed due to lack of
oxygen. Almost 12,000 houses were ruined, along with banks, shops,

warehouses, factories, churches, hospitals and the zoo. The attacks were justified by the Allies as a legitimate assault on a military and industrial target, with newspapers also reporting on damage to rail communications, which would hinder the movement of German armies.

The grim and horrifying reality of Nazi concentration camps was brought under the public gaze in April. As Allied troops marched through formerly German-occupied areas liberating the camps, a true picture of events there came to light. The details of atrocities are today well known and need not be detailed too graphically here. British newspapers and radio broadcasts told of how the men discovered piles of dead bodies, evidence of torture, people in advanced stages of starvation, primitive, filthy accommodation and widespread illness. Buchenwald, near Weimar in Germany, was the first camp liberated by US troops, although before their arrival thousands had been forced to take part in evacuation marches as the Nazis attempted to remove evidence of their crimes. On 11 April, the US Third Army reached the camp and was accompanied by several journalists who faced the difficult and unenviable task of describing what they found there to those at home. Around 21,000 inmates were technically released, although some were too ill or weak to move and deaths continued despite the administering of aid. Reports at the time estimated that around 60,000 had perished there during the war.

As more and more camps were liberated, descriptions of conditions continued to run, sometimes simply substituted by harrowing photographs. Death tolls mounted, and around the world people struggled to comprehend the extent of what had happened.

Peace is Announced

Victory for the Allies, and all those overseas and on the home front, finally came on 8 May, 1945. Known as VE – Victory in Europe – Day, 8 May marked the unconditional surrender of Nazi Germany and was celebrated all around the world. The vast empire that Hitler had sought to create, the legions of proud marching soldiers and the regime of fear, had fallen and was in ruins. King George VI, Queen Elizabeth, their daughters the princesses Elizabeth (the future Queen

Elizabeth II) and Margaret, and Prime Minister Winston Churchill stood on the balcony of Buckingham Palace above crowds of cheering people as the nation poured onto the streets to celebrate. The news of victory, when it finally came, seemed long overdue. In fact, expectant crowds had gathered outside the palace on 7 May in anticipation of an announcement of peace that didn't come. Some houses were already decked in bunting, ready for the official end of the war. At 7.40 p.m. on that evening, a radio bulletin finally broadcast the news: the following day would be VE Day. While the news was expected, it was no less exciting for it. At 3 p.m. on 8 May, Winston Churchill took to the radio waves from 10 Downing Street to declare the coming of peace, telling the jubilant nation, 'This is your victory.'

The BBC ran ten days of victory radio programmes as a celebration, including a special episode of *ITMA*: the much-beloved comedy *It's That Man Again*. Street celebrations broke out everywhere, and over 1 million people gathered in the centre of London, where bombs once fell at a terrifying rate. In some popular areas, those in crowds could hardly move, and the sea of bodies was bright with the red, white and blue of the Union Jack flag. Church bells rang out far and wide and street lights shone in sharp contrast to the darkness of the war and the blackout. For the first time since the war began, notable public buildings such as Broadcasting House and the Houses of Parliament were floodlit. Even the princesses Elizabeth and Margaret took part in the fun; wanting to join with the crowds, they slipped out of Buckingham Palace and stood outside it to see their parents address the masses. Later, in 1985, Queen Elizabeth II would describe it as 'one of the most memorable nights of my life'. An estimated 50,000 people were still celebrating in London's Piccadilly Circus at midnight. In Cardiff, around 30,000 gathered together in the city centre to hear the Prime Minister speak over the radio. In Nottingham, effigies of Hitler and Mussolini were burned.

In a speech broadcast over the radio, King George VI, addressed his people with the victorious words, 'Germany, the enemy who drove all Europe into war, has been finally overcome.'

What mustn't be forgotten is the crippling effect that the war had on the nations that Britain had been fighting with and against. Countless German civilians died in RAF bombing raids on German cities; the total number of civilian deaths is estimated at somewhere between 1 million and 2,500,000. Between 12 and 15 million Soviet Union civilians died between 1939 and 1945. Though every life lost is equally tragic, the total civilian deaths in the United Kingdom amounted to just over 67,000. At the end of the war, countries such as Germany were – in many places – quite literally in ruins. In Germany, food was scarce for many years, heavy industry was removed and prisoners of war and civilians were forced into hard labour as punishment. Shipments of food were sent from the United States to keep the country going, but nutrition was poor and death rates rose.

While VE Day marked the end of hostilities in Europe, the war was not over in Japan. In his victory speech, Churchill announced, 'We may allow ourselves a brief period of rejoicing; but let us not forget for a moment the toil and efforts that lie ahead. Japan, with all her treachery and greed, remains unsubdued. The injury she has inflicted on Great Britain, the United States and other countries, and her detestable cruelties, call for justice and retribution.'

Retribution did certainly come. At 8.15 a.m. on 6 August 1945, the US dropped the first atomic bomb on Hiroshima, one of the chief supply areas for the Japanese army and a key shipping location. Known as 'Little Boy', the bomb was said to be more than 2,000 times more destructive than any bomb previously used. Over 60 per cent of the city was destroyed, and almost 150,000 people killed, some immediately and others from radiation. Such devastation had never been seen on this scale before. Where houses had once stood, the ground was like a wasteland. Clothes were vaporised off the backs of their wearers. Three days later, a second atomic bomb was dropped on Japan, this time on the city of Nagasaki on the island of Kyushu, a prime location for ship-building and a supplier of vessels to the Imperial Japanese Navy. At 11.02 a.m. on 9 August, an atomic bomb code-named 'Fat Man' was dropped on the north of the city, directly killing 70,000 people. On 15 August, VJ (Victory over Japan) Day took place, as Japan finally surrendered to the Allies. In America, large-scale celebrations took place. Crowds gathered in Times Square and a mass of people even attempted to break into the grounds of the White House. A two-day holiday was granted in the UK, US and Australia and American President Harry S. Truman declared it 'the day when fascism finally dies'. King George VI said, 'Our hearts are full to overflowing, as are your own. Yet there is not one of us who has experienced this terrible war who does not realise that we shall feel its inevitable consequences long after we have all forgotten our rejoicings today.'

After the War

My wartime experiment ends with 1945 but, for those really living on the home front, the end of the Second World War didn't spell the end of rationing and shortages. Certainly, some products were more readily available and utility items gradually fell out of fashion as more desirable alternatives were put forward. As ever, food was one of the areas in which the greatest shortfall was found, and staple items such as butter, margarine, cheese and meat continued to be rationed for years afterwards. Coming off the ration was a lengthy process. In most cases, the amounts of each food allowed per person were slowly increased until availability reached a point at which it could be sold without restriction.

Preserves such as jam and marmalade were de-rationed in December 1948, but it would be almost four years until the next item, tea, was de-rationed in October 1952. Throughout 1953, food continued to be de-rationed, including sweets and sugar. Other items, such as cream and different varieties of cheese, became available once again after vanishing from the consumer market during the wartime years. During the war, milk supplies had been channelled into producing just one variety of cheese, which was the type subjected to rationing. After 1945, other specialist varieties began to be produced, but were controlled by a points scheme.

Some items, such as bread, were actually rationed for the first time during the post-war years. Throughout the war, the National Loaf had been an essential part of every person's diet, but in 1946 fears of widespread famine in many countries led to the introduction of a bread ration. In April 1946, the government announced that it was prepared to ration bread in the UK if a similar scheme was adopted in the US, to help improve wheat and flour supplies in countries such as Poland, Italy and Greece. Britain was part of a Combined Food Board, which also included the US and Canada and controlled the distribution of cereals around the world. Prime Minister Clement Attlee, speaking in the House of Commons, proposed that the best option for weathering the storm was for all countries to share their resources for the common good, as they had done during the war. Former Prime Minister Winston Churchill was strongly opposed to the idea, as was a large proportion of the British public. Churchill described the announcement of bread rationing as 'one of the gravest I have ever heard in time of peace'. After years of austerity, this final measure seemed a bridge too far. Nevertheless, bread rationing went ahead, beginning on 21 July. The basic adult ration was nine bread 'units' per week, with a large loaf being worth four units and one pound of flour being three units. Cakes, flour, buns and scones were also included as part of the 'bread' ration. This equated to a proposed daily ration of 9 oz, or six medium-thickness slices. The ration for children was calculated according to age, with children aged eleven to eighteen years being entitled to more bread than an adult. Expectant mothers and male and female manual workers also received more. The scheme remained in place for two years until July 1948.

Rationing officially ended in 1954, with fats rationing ceasing on 8 May. After this, branded margarine was manufactured for the first time in years; during the war, only a 'national' margarine was available. Instead of one flat price, more expensive alternatives could be sold alongside the standard product. At the end of June, the Ministry of Food ceased work in its slaughterhouses and private meat production began once again. Meat and bacon were the last items to be de-rationed at midnight, 3 July 1954. 'D [De-rationing] Day' was celebrated across the country, with ration books being burned. Around 500 books were burned by a prospective MP at a Conservative fete in Middlesex.

In total, rationing controlled the nation's diet for over fourteen years, with some children growing up having never known a different way of life. Shops now had a greater variety of foods, as well as more of them. The nation, delighted by the freedom to use butter, flour and eggs when it liked, embraced baking once again. While it was loathed by most people at one time, the wartime rationing system had in many ways been a positive thing. With supply uncertain and stocks low, rationing was an effective way of reassuring people that they would always have enough food to get by. While quantities may be small and variety poor, if the entire ration entitlement was claimed each week and meals were carefully planned with no wastage, everybody – rich and poor alike – could survive on what they had. Price controlling meant that high demand for goods could not be matched by high prices, which would have excluded those with less money. Immediately after the end of meat rationing, prices soared as demand escalated. Points rationing for tinned and dried goods allowed everyone to have items additional to the basic ration, but forced them to choose those they desired most, rather than making everything available but at an inflated price. Great time and effort was put into educating Britain about health and nutrition and many who could not cook before the war were trained to make nourishing meals from scratch. Certainly, food rationing had its flaws, but it also had numerous positive outcomes, which are often forgotten by those of us looking back into history.

Demobilisation

For many women, the end of the war was a bittersweet experience. Housewives, used only to cooking, cleaning and bringing up children, had been given a glimpse of a different life, in which they could have a career of their own. Admittedly, the jobs women did during the war were not all glamorous and liberating. They could be repetitive, tedious and back-breaking. But equally, the pressure of working while maintaining a home proved to women that they could do more than they had ever thought. War work could be challenging: former dish-washers found themselves operating heavy machinery, ploughing fields and making Lancaster bombers. Some held ranks higher than men and were put in the position of issuing orders. In posters encouraging women to take up wartime service, the workers portrayed looked healthy, happy and entirely self-assured. It was no longer attractively feminine to be weak and delicate; strength and confidence in adversity won through. Having a job separate to the domestic sphere fostered a sense of independence that some women had never known, and that others had left behind when they married. The environment of war also broke down social conventions and led to a greater amount of freedom.

However, within months, women – particularly married women – went from being a truly valuable and valued part of Britain's military and labour force, to being out of work. While the female population had done an admirable job, they had, in the eyes of society's decision-makers, simply been standing in for men who were now returning. While some female industry continued in the post-war years – the Women's Land Army, for instance – many were wound up soon after victory, with demobilisation beginning in June 1945. The Women's Timber Corps was disbanded in 1946.

It was thought that, domestically, things might return to the way they had been before the outbreak of war. This was not necessarily so. In the years following, divorce rates rose at a rapid rate and murmurs of discontent grew louder. In the 1950s and 60s, these murmurs grew to a roar as feminism reached fever pitch. However slow the progress, the dynamic between men and women would eventually change.

Month Twelve

Day 360
I have just harvested my first very small parsnip and, to my disappointment, found it complete with a hanger-on: inside the top of it was a grub, which had eaten into it just below the soil and right down through the middle. Now that this has happened, I faintly remember being warned of the risk by a gardening expert many months ago. There's nothing like hindsight to make you feel cranky.

Day 363
It's very strange to think that my year of living in the Second World War is almost over. The end seems to have crept up on me; after months of counting the days left, suddenly there are fewer than I thought. To my amazement, I actually feel a bit sad that the experience is coming to an end and feel something close to nostalgia for the time, just under a year ago, when I was starting out and struggling to adapt to all the changes in lifestyle. I think the main reason that I am so surprised I've almost finished is that in many ways, on a day-to-day basis, I have forgotten that the way I live now is not just normal life. Obviously, there are elements of wartime life that are

still strange, weighing out weekly rations being the most obvious. But other things, such as not eating white bread, pre-made meals or imported (i.e. out-of-season) fruit and vegetables, have become perfectly normal to me. I know that there are aspects of modern life that I will probably continue to shun, even when I return to living in the twenty-first century. I now can't see myself buying vegetables that are imported from distant climes, particularly when they are things that can just as easily be grown in this country. I also look forward to continuing to listen to the radio as I have done for the last year; this has been such a lifeline during the 'war' and I've come to love sitting quietly and tuning in.

Of course, there are some things from modern life that I can't wait to revisit. I love cheese, and one of my first purchases will definitely be a good selection of different cheeses. It'll also be lovely to sit down with a steak and not feel guilty at using my entire meat ration in one meal. I've enjoyed discovering more of the literature written pre-1945, but it'll be nice to treat myself to a couple of modern novels. One amusing side-effect of this experiment, recently pointed out, is that apparently my diet of wartime books, newspapers and films has led me to occasionally lapse into using old-fashioned language and phrases when I speak. I don't notice I'm doing it, but odd remarks can induce much hilarity in everyone else.

Recipe Card: Eggless Chocolate Cake

This cake would have been perfect for a street party, as it doesn't use too many rations but could serve several people, including children.

Ingredients:
3 oz (85 g) margarine
3 oz (110 g) sugar
6 oz (175 g) self-raising flour
1 oz (25 g) cocoa powder
¼ pint (150 ml) milk
1 tbsp golden syrup
1 tsp baking powder
½ tsp vanilla essence

Method:

Preheat the oven to 190°C/Gas Mark 5. Line a medium-sized cake tin with greaseproof paper (if available), or grease it very well.

Cream together the margarine, sugar and golden syrup until fluffy and light. Gradually fold in the flour and cocoa powder, sifted together, and then add the vanilla essence and milk. Mix together until you have a smooth mixture, and spoon into the cake tin.

Bake in the oven for around fifteen minutes, or until a skewer inserted in the cake comes out clean. Allow to cool slightly in the cake tin before removing it and placing on a wire rack to cool properly.

If you have the extra rations available, an icing for the top of the cake can be made by melting two teaspoons of margarine and mixing this with one tablespoon of cocoa, one tablespoon of golden syrup and a couple of drops of vanilla essence.

After the War

Back to Modern Life: Day Two

It's hard to comprehend that my wartime experiment is over and I can live in the twenty-first century again. To be honest, I've done very little differently since my wartime year ended. Yesterday, as a celebration, I bought two bananas and some breakfast cereal. I haven't had cereal since the very beginning of the war as it was in short supply and the more patriotic option was porridge oats, which didn't have to be imported. After a year of eating porridge, I am very keen to move onto something else. Aside from these two purchases, I'm doing little differently. I spent a fairly generous amount of time thinking about foodstuffs that I could buy and decided that I don't really need anything wild and exotic; my wartime larder is quite well-stocked with staples – I've got vegetables, and I don't want to feel like I'm buying modern food just for the sake of it.

Watching television (not lots, just one programme) also makes me feel guilty, as if I'm doing something that I shouldn't. I keep forgetting that the wartime period has ended and it isn't breaking the rules now, but there is still an ingrained association between television and guilt. Having painfully broken my pre-war routine of watching television all the time, I'm going to be careful not to force myself back into it.

Instead, this evening I am knitting and reading (not at the same time, of course). If truth be told, I'm finding the end of the war a bit of an anti-climax and think that I am going to have some trouble adjusting to modern living.

Two Weeks Later

Today, with supplies running a little low, I did my first proper post-war grocery shop, which I can only describe as an intensely strange experience. I have become used to ignoring whole aisles in the supermarket, ones which contain items that I would never be able to buy on a wartime diet. I had walked part of the way around the shop before it occurred to me that I was actually allowed to buy anything I liked – like a child being let free in a sweet shop. It wasn't that I actually wanted to buy a lot of the things I saw; it was just the strangest of feelings, knowing that I could. Consequently I embarked on a period of mental turmoil and self-goading, whereby I stopped in front of particularly 'un-wartime' foods and looked at them for a long time, gazing from all angles and reading all the ingredients before deciding if they would make it into the trolley. Most items didn't make it. One surprising realisation (or perhaps, if I think hard about it, it isn't that surprising) was that I seem to have become fussier about what I will and will not buy since living for a year on rations. Food seems to have acquired a greater importance and value, and I am no longer willing to spend my money on items that I don't think are worth it.

In the end, I allowed my 'child in a sweet shop' alter ego to buy a few luxury post-war items. Into the trolley went olives, yoghurts, tortelloni, pesto and couscous. By the time I reached the checkout, feeling excited about my meals for the coming week, I had remembered a valuable – literally valuable – lesson from my wartime year. Rationing makes your weekly shop far cheaper. My post-war splurge came with a post-war price tag. In all, my groceries for this week cost double what I'd spend on an average 'wartime' shop. I'm not going to deny myself the odd treat now and again, but after having a celebratory week or two, I may well try to revert to some adapted version of a wartime diet for the future. Austerity bites, but we could all do a lot worse.

Things I Have Learned:

1 Even a humble outdoor planting area can produce a reasonable harvest and supplement a supermarket shop.
2 The hedgerows are more bountiful than we may think – and our ancestors had the right idea with country wines.
3 With a little ingenuity, most waste needn't be waste at all and can be reused at least once.
4 A lot of modern things are unnecessary: sliced bread, pre-packed salad, fruit from Kenya, vegetables from Israel. Just because you can have it when you want it, doesn't mean you should.
5 Potatoes are an unlikely superfood, as well as being versatile and cheap.
6 A wartime grocery basket costs less than a modern-day one. Staples in the larder make it cheaper to buy supplementary items.
7 By removing modern distractions such as the internet and television, simple pleasures, such as crafts, reading and puzzles, are more enjoyable and, ultimately, life becomes more productive.
8 It's not necessarily a good thing to have access to everything you want all the time. A little self-discipline can be a surprisingly liberating thing.
9 Faster is seldom better. Speed can equal stress.

Some of the More Trivial Things I Have Learned

1 Leaf tea tastes better than teabags.
2 Knitting makes your wrists ache after a while.
3 Buying fruit and vegetables in season can actually be quite exciting.
4 As a follow-on to the above point, broccoli tastes far better after an absence of six months.
5 Gorse flower should be thoroughly fermented out before it is bottled or it may explode and induce heart attacks.
6 Potato crop failures can make you cry.
7 Waiting for jam to set can be a fraught process.

In the Kitchen Garden

Things to Do:
January
This may well be a fallow month, but there are still things that can be done to keep your vegetable patch ticking over. Continue to harvest winter crops such as brassicas, and plan out your planting scheme for the coming year, with spaces allocated for each thing. If you have the space to create three or four separate planting zones for rotation, this should result in healthier produce in the long term.

While growing conditions are at a low, continue with previous winter tasks: tackle weeds and clear the spaces that you'll want to use in spring. Keep everything in good order – mend fencing, check your shed is watertight and if you have a greenhouse make sure that the glass is secure and hasn't been disturbed by winter winds. On a dry day (not after rain), dig over the soil in your garden. This will bring any potential crop-eating pests to the surface and provide a food source for hungry birds at the same time.

Conclusion

It might seem, from reading this book, that I imply that modern life is awful, and that the Second World War was a better time. This is certainly not my point. Modern life has many advantages over the 1940s – in fact, too many to mention – but progress doesn't have to mean throwing away everything that came before in order to be different. A rejection of traditional values isn't essential to creating a healthy, progressive society. Some elements of our past are worth keeping. The drive to buy less and use more is something that should definitely form part of everyday life today. Wartime years have proven cheaper, with less waste – not just of food, but of everything. Not having every possible item to hand, whether this is in creating a dish or a piece of gardening equipment, leads to far more experimentation and innovation. One of the main things I have learned is that we don't need half of the things we have.

The real conclusion to this book is in its introduction. The reasons that I originally wanted to take up this investigation remain the reasons that I now think it was worthwhile. Living for a whole year as if it were the Second World War might seem an overly drastic way of gaining a new perspective on life, but there is no denying that the experience has taught me a lot and offered an incredibly valuable insight into a life very different from ours. There were probably elements of the reconstruction that were deeply flawed, and I'm sure that I didn't always do everything right. Of course, there is no way that anyone could accurately replicate the home-front life nowadays; at least, not without an awful lot of money and access to special effects. But at times, my makeshift encounter felt that it might in some way be genuine. Though self-imposed, there was deprivation, frustration and disappointment. I'm not sorry I did it, though at times during the process, I was. The last year has allowed me to push myself in new ways and to discover things that I might not have done otherwise. I've learned that I can create meals from the bare minimum of ingredients, and I've begun to understand what is in season locally at different times of the year and what I am capable of growing or making myself. With less distraction from endless sources of immediate entertainment, I have been more productive and uncovered new ways of spending my time. I enjoy watching television and playing games on my computer, and this will probably never change, but 'going cold turkey' from these pursuits made me realise how much time and effort we now put into wasting time. Hours upon hours of every day are spent taking a break from life, as it breezes past us.

I'm not saying that we shouldn't watch television, or order takeaways, or eat tropical fruit. I don't want this book to become the sanctimonious lecture of a traditionalist. I wouldn't necessarily recommend that anyone reading this spends a year cutting themselves off from modern society. However, I'd be the first to advocate taking small steps to explore the home-front ethos. Take a night off from electronics, cook an entirely seasonal meal, grow a pot of salad or do something within the community. Much has changed for the better since the Second World War, and we can be grateful that we are no longer in the situation in which 1940s families found themselves. But let us not forget them, or what they did, entirely.